Why You Get Rejected

Why You Get Rejected

**HOW TO CRAFT THE PERFECT COLLEGE APPLICATION
(BY GIVING COLLEGES WHAT THEY ACTUALLY WANT)**

Anthony-James Green

ISBN-13: 9781530214693
ISBN-10: 1530214696
Library of Congress Control Number: 2016903320
CreateSpace Independent Publishing Platform
North Charleston, South Carolina

Table of Contents

Section One: Introduction

Where I change the way that you think about the entire application process.

CHAPTER 1

What Do Colleges Really Want?

> *"Ask not what your college can do for you, but what you can do for your college."*
> — THE ONLY COLLEGE APPLICATION ADVICE YOU'LL EVER REALLY NEED

I f you take only one idea from this book, take this: colleges are selfish.

Colleges are the seat and wellspring of our academic future. They provide boundless educational opportunities, resources, and experiences to their students - even those students who could never otherwise afford these gifts. They mold the minds and sharpen the skills of our nation's most promising youths. And, above all else, they are completely, utterly, and profoundly selfish.

Keep something in mind - when I say *selfish*, I don't mean *evil*. Not selfish in the Ebenezer Scrooge sense of the word. I simply mean that colleges can't help anyone else until they've first ensured their own survival. In the long run, colleges survive and thrive in only one way: by letting in the right students - the students who can *contribute the most to the college*. People are so caught up in *what they'll get from college* that they rarely, if ever, realize the more important truth: the entire college admissions system is designed to select *the students who can give the most to colleges*. Admissions officers simply weed out the least useful applicants until the most productive ones remain.

Want to get into the college of your dreams? Simply prove yourself useful enough to avoid being weeded out.

Remember: *colleges are run by human beings*. There is no such thing as "Harvard University" - it, like all other colleges, is an abstract concept. Harvard is simply a collection of human beings tasked with keeping this abstract concept alive, in charge of giant trusts and bank accounts that fund the concept, living and working in buildings that are owned by these trusts, and educating students who identify with the concept, contribute to the concept, and ultimately make or break the reputation of the concept.

Harvard can't make decisions. Only the people in charge of Harvard can make decisions. And they make decisions the same way that all humans do: based on their own self-interests. While all reputable universities are *not-for-profit*, this does NOT mean that they're *charities*. There is a large difference between the two.

Colleges do a tremendous amount of good in this world, but they can't accomplish much unless their own needs are taken care of first. If you've ever been in an airplane, you already know the drill: before you put the oxygen mask on your kid...

Just as no mother can help her children to breathe without getting oxygen herself, no college can help its students and the surrounding community without its own "oxygen." So what do colleges *breathe*? Only two things, actually:

1. **Money.**
2. **Reputation.**

In essence, these two elements are part of one cycle. Colleges need money to fund their operations, and in the long run, they need excellent reputations to keep collecting money. The better their reputations, the more money they get. So long as they have money, they survive and expand. Money leads to better classes, more buildings, bigger campuses, bigger-name instructors, better football coaches - you name it. If a college has more money, it becomes a better college. This leads to a better reputation. A better reputation leads to even more money... the cycle continues ad infinitum.

There are only three ways that colleges can make money. Depending on the college, the ratios between these three can vary wildly. They are:

1. **Tuition**
2. **Donations**
3. **Peripheral Sources**

The first two are self-explanatory. "Peripheral sources" are research grants, patents, television rights for their sports programs, and any other source of income other than tuition and direct donations.

The better the reputation of the college, the more of all three they'll be able to obtain. So what plays into the reputation of any college? Let's start with the obvious stuff: The US News and World Report ranking system is considered gospel by pretty much every parent in the world. Sure, there are those who claim that these rankings are irrelevant, but they're the same people who attend/work for/promote the colleges with the lowest rankings on this and similar lists.

So how do colleges improve their reputations and their rankings in systems such as the US News and World Report and Forbes?

The big factors are pretty straightforward:

- The average GPA of their incoming students
- The average SAT/ACT scores of their incoming students
- The percentage of applicants who gain admission
- The percentage of admitted applicants who actually attend
- The amount that their average graduate donates to the school (see a pattern developing here?)
- The % of their graduates that consistently donate (the cycle continues)
- Class sizes (more money = less need to stuff classes with extra students)
- Average exiting salary and employment rate of their graduates (which leads to larger donations)
- Average % of graduate acceptance to top-tier grad schools (which lead to even higher-paying jobs)
- Research grants and accolades awarded (i.e., the rich get richer)
- Quality of teachers, staff, and resources (and guess what buys high-quality staff and resources?)

There's an endless cycle here. Money buys good rankings, and good rankings bring in more money. Yet the colleges, in and of themselves, have no power to generate money. They're only as good as the students who attend (and want to attend) them.

This is where you, the applicant, come in. You've been so focused on *what the school can do for you*, and what it would mean if you got accepted, that you haven't been looking at things the right way. In reality, **these schools need you just as much, if not more, than you need them** - but *only if you can enhance their reputations or get them more money.*

So how does this rule help you to improve your college application? By understanding something very simple:

> **The ONLY way to get into *any* college is to prove that you will do *more* to enhance the school's monetary and/or reputational resources than will *all the students whom the college is forced to reject.***

Once you understand this, you'll be able to think about your application in the proper light. You're not trying to *get in* - you're trying to *avoid the chopping block* by promising more potential worth to admissions officers than your fellow applicants. Colleges don't accept you simply "because you're smart" - they want smart people because they'll contribute to the school's reputation and coffers. They don't accept you "because you're a good person" - they want good people because they'll enhance the reputation of the school.

This book aims to teach you one thing: how to use your application to prove your potential worth to college admissions officers. No more, no less. In the pages that follow, I'll show you what college admissions officers are looking for in an application, along with the giant red flags that'll get your application tossed in the trash. Crafting a winning application isn't rocket science, but it *does* require a proper understanding of how colleges think, what they're looking for, and what's sure to get you rejected.

Now that you have a basic idea of what colleges *actually* want, I can show you how to present it to them in your application, to craft a perfect college resume, and to avoid all the biggest application mistakes by teaching you *why you get rejected.*

CHAPTER 2

A Small Hole Sinks a Big Ship (and the Dating Game)

Throughout this book, I'll be making consistent comparisons between *applying to college* and *dating*. The first time you see a potential date at the coffee shop = the first time a college glances at your application. Marriage = getting accepted. Though it might seem silly at first, the analogy is much more accurate than you might realize.

When you're looking for a potential mate, the first requirement is that *you like what you see*. If someone clearly hasn't showered for a week, or they're wearing a T-shirt that says "I Like to Kill Stuff," the conversation probably isn't going anywhere. In the same way, if a student's application *looks* horrible (bad grades, bad scores, missing elements), it's not even going to get read.

Once we like what we see, we start caring about personality. No one needs to date a supermodel - we're just looking for someone *good-looking enough for us.* Once that threshold is passed, personality is all that matters, and appearance doesn't play much of a role anymore. Your "personality" is *everything in your application other than your grades and test scores:* your essays, recommendations, extracurriculars, etc.

It doesn't matter if you're the best looking person in the world - if you have zero personality, you're not going to have a happy marriage. In the same way, it doesn't matter if you have a 2400 SAT score and a 4.2 weighted GPA if you have *nothing else going for you* - unless, of course, you're marrying a very *shallow* person (i.e., a school that's so desperate for high numbers that it'll marry you for high metrics alone).

And, just like budding relationships, college applications are extremely fragile. Once two people are married, they can chew with their mouths open and forget to take out the trash without getting divorced. But if someone passes gas at the table on the *first date*, it's probably a deal breaker.

You need to imagine yourself as "courting" your colleges. Just as a tiny mistake on the first date can kill any chances of a long-term relationship, so the tiniest mistakes on your application can get it tossed in the trash. The earlier in the application process you mess up, the bigger a deal that mistake will be.

Sure, you might be a great person, and you might have just made one tiny, little mistake, but here's the problem: there are *thousands* of other people courting this same college, and *none of them passed gas at the dinner table on the first date*. Which brings us to perhaps the most important thing you need to realize about college applications:

Applications do not happen in a vacuum - they are about COMPARISON. You're not proving your own absolute value - you're proving that you're *better than everyone else*. It doesn't matter how *good* you are - it matters how *comparatively good* you are.

I once had a conversation with a potential client (whom I didn't end up taking on) whose son had been suspended from school for, basically, a hate crime. He had written an *extremely* racially insensitive message on another student's wall, gotten caught, and been kicked out of school for a term. His mother wanted to know if he had any chances of getting into a competitive school, and argued her case thusly:

> Look, I know that what he did was wrong. But overall, he's a great kid. He's an awesome athlete, has a 3.9 GPA, and with your help, he'll be able to get a 2200+ on the SAT. He's also going to get great recommendations from a lot of his teachers, and he's a good essay writer. You still think he has a strong shot, right?

My answer to her: *no*

My longer answer: your kid might, "*overall*," be a great kid. But any school he applies to is going to have *thousands* of other applicants who *didn't commit hate crimes*. He has a 0% chance of getting into a competitive college. Sorry.

Again, let's go back to the dating analogy. Imagine you're at a speed-dating event. You have literally thousands of eligible people who you might be able to date. You meet someone who's good-looking, charming, etc., and 5 minutes into the date, he/she says:

"Well, it's a funny story, but last year, I sort of committed a hate crime! Anyway, aside from that, my hobbies include...."

AXED.

Remember again: admissions are about **comparison**, and not about **absolute value**. It's not as if "hate crimes deduct 10 points from an application, but strong SAT scores add 11, so they sort of balance each other out." This isn't how it works.

When something really ugly shows up on your application, you don't get "points deducted" - you get chopped. There's a point of no return.

Also remember: *colleges care about reputation more than anything else in the world.* What do you think a student with a drunk driving offense, or a hate crime, or any other sort of horrendous offense, is going to do for a college's reputation?

Schools do NOT like to take *downside risks* - only upside risks. Most colleges let in thousands of students each year, which means that they have to have pretty "diversi-fied portfolios." But they're not in the business of losing money. While schools might "gamble on" a student who has a lot of potential *upside*, they will NEVER gamble on a student who has any potential *downside*.

In other words: if you can convince colleges that you *might* do something really awe-some, they *might* let you in - above and beyond the students who have slightly better grades and scores than you. But if you hint to a college that you might do something horrendous, you're in bad shape.

"Yeah, sure," you might say, "but I haven't committed a hate crime or been caught drunk driving- so why does this apply to me?"

Excellent question. The answer:

Students do NOT get admitted to college - they AVOID BEING CHOPPED.

At first, this might seem like a pretty obvious statement. *Getting accepted* is exactly the same thing as *not getting rejected.* But to think about the college application game properly, you need to work under this framework: *you aren't trying to "get in" - you're trying to "survive."*

Obviously, major infractions such as hate crimes, drunk driving offenses, school expulsions, etc., look bad, but they're far from the only things that get you chopped.

Some of the others:

- Bad grades
- Bad test scores
- Lack of extracurricular activities
- Lack of (or bad) recommendations
- Failure to demonstrate interest in the college
- Simple application errors
- Failure to pick a "right fit" college
- Bad essay(s)
- Many more

This book will teach you how to avoid all of the above. By the time you're finished, you'll understand *exactly* how to craft a perfect college application. You'll do that by offering schools precisely what they want, and, just as importantly, by avoiding the many errors that'll get your application eliminated.

A small hole can sink a massive ship. Rather than provide you with useless "to do" items that *don't address your fundamental application errors*, I'm going to start by *patching up the holes in the hull*. Doing extra "goodies" when your application is fundamentally flawed is like rearranging the deck chairs on the Titanic. Hence, we'll start with the fundamentals, and *then* we get into the "tips and tricks" that'll sweeten the pot for admissions officers.

If we're on the same page so far, and you're ready to think about college in this way, it's time to begin!

CHAPTER 3

College is What You Make of It (and It's a Crapshoot)

n every martial arts class, the first lesson is dedicated to a very specific concept: "we won't teach you a single move until you accept what you should (and should not) be using these moves for." Before you learn how to chop a brick in half, you *first* need to understand that you shouldn't be chopping *people* in half unless you're defending yourself. There's a right and a wrong way to use any skill.

Before you learn the material within this book, I have to make a similar disclaimer. This book will help you get into more, better colleges than you would have been able to previously. But you need to understand two things before you use the knowledge within:

1. **The term "better" is HIGHLY subjective.**
2. **No matter how amazing your application might be, college applications are ALWAYS a crapshoot.**

I'm a living embodiment of both points. I went to one of the "best" schools in the country. Unfortunately, it wasn't *best for me*.

I've always been a guy who loves small, tight-knit communities, who enjoys knowing everyone and being known by everyone, and who likes to get involved in as many aspects of my school as possible.

I like one-on-one lessons much more than I like classroom lectures. I'm extremely Type-A, but I always feel happiest, calmest, and most productive when I'm surrounded by nature. I should have gone to a small, community-based liberal arts college with small classes, tons of school spirit, and a lot of natural activities.

Instead, I drank "the ranking Kool-Aid" and went to Columbia University.

I got a lot out of Columbia, and it was a fantastic experience in many ways. Columbia "throws you to the wolves." It teaches you to grow up and be an adult - or else.

Columbia teaches you the value of a buck, since you're always worried about money in a city-school environment. More than anything, it teaches you to work your tail off at all times of the day and night. I think Columbia quintupled my work ethic and was largely responsible for the launch of my first company. But I want to make one thing clear:

I was not happy at Columbia.

Some people were thrilled to be there. They loved the large lecture environment, the hyper-independent atmosphere, and the Manhattan pace of life. It was the perfect school for them. But it wasn't the perfect school for me. I went to Columbia over all the other schools I was admitted to for one reason, and one reason only: it had the highest rank in *US News & World Report*.

When you're going through the college selection process, I need you to realize something: the rank of your school has little to do with how successful you're going to be in life. And it has *nothing* to do with how happy you're going to be as a person.

I've met people who attended colleges I've never heard of who run *multi-million dollar businesses*, who work for the best consulting and legal firms in the nation, and who have saliva-inducing jobs at some of the best production studios and media firms in the world. I've known social outcasts who go to the right college and end up meeting like-minded people and becoming total social butterflies.

I also know half-suicidal Harvard grads, and I have classmates who are still unemployed nearly seven years after graduation, or who work as bartenders paying off $200,000+ in student loan debt. Of course, I also know plenty of extremely successful Columbia and Harvard grads who were very happy during their undergraduate experience. My only point is this:

College is what you make of it. If you go to a top-ten college, it doesn't mean you'll be a success, and if you go to a no-name college, it doesn't mean you'll be a failure. The activities, students, faculty, environment, and opportunities provided by each college can be seized or ignored by every student, and only those students who seize as many opportunities as possible will end up happy, fulfilled, and successful.

As you read through this book, you'll notice that I'm rather "tough-love." I'm not like this because I think you need to go to an Ivy League to be worth a damn. I'm like this because **a good application gives you options, and the more options you have, the more likely it is that you'll be able to go to a school that's right for you.** That's it. So as you read on, be sure to realize that a perfect application is a means to an end, and that end is **options, not rankings.**

For some students, Pomona would be an absolute dream, and Cal Tech would be a living hell. For other students, quite the opposite is true. But you're not getting into either school without a fantastic application.

I'll show you exactly how to research your target colleges, find more, and craft a list of places where you'll truly *develop as a person, use your talents*, and *receive the best educational experience possible*. If you're only reading this book to get into a rank-superior school, you're like a guy taking karate so that he can beat up strangers at the bar. You're taking the right lessons for the wrong reasons. Find the college **that's right for you** - NOT the college that has the best name recognition at a cocktail party.

College Applications Are a Crapshoot

Oftentimes, I'm asked questions such as this:

> *"My kid has a 4.2 weighted GPA, he's a star soccer player, and he got 99th percentile SAT scores. He also started a charity that raised over $500,000 for underprivileged children. He'll get into Princeton, right?"*

My answer is always the same:

> "Maybe."

There is no such thing as a guaranteed admission to ANY school, no matter how good of an applicant you happen to be.

If that same parent has asked me the following:

> *"My kid has a 4.2 weighted GPA, he's a star soccer player, got 99th percentile SAT scores, and started a charity that raised over $500,000 for underprivileged children. If he applies to Princeton, Harvard, Columbia, Brown, Penn, Pomona, Cal Tech, Vanderbilt, Duke, Berkeley, USC, Amherst, Williams, and Middlebury, he'll get into at least one of those schools, right?"*

My answer would be:

> "Very likely so."

Before you begin this process, you have to realize something essential:

You should NEVER put all of your eggs in one college basket. Ever.

Saying things such as:

> *"If I don't go to UVA, I'm a failure!"*

Or:

> *"Johnny absolutely must go to Amherst - it's the only school for him!"*

Aren't just foolish - they're also devastating to your own psychology, and completely unrealistic.

Imagine going to a casino and rolling a di. You're betting that it'll land on 1, 2, 3, 4, or 5. You say to the dealer, "if I don't win, I'm going to *kill you!*" Anyone around you would probably start beckoning security. Well, it's just as ridiculous and counterproductive to do the same thing when it comes to college admissions. Find a *range of schools that'll give you exactly what you're looking for from an educational experience* and apply to all of them. That way, no matter where you end up, you'll get what you want. But saying that "you'll only be happy if you go to Harvard" is unrealistic and ridiculous. As if the only happy or successful people in the world are the people who went to one specific university.

When I applied early, I went for Brown. I had fantastic SAT scores, I was the co-editor of my school's comedy paper, and I was a highly sought after crew recruit. According to the crew coach at Brown, I was basically a sure thing.

Except that I wasn't. I was rejected. As it turns out, he basically lied to me and told me that I was being recruited when I wasn't, hoping that I'd get in anyway and still be loyal to the crew program. That way, he could use his "recruitment silver bullets" on kids with worse applications than mine. He could have his cake and eat it, too.

At the time, it was devastating. I ended up applying to sixteen additional schools for my regular round of admissions. Without going into all the details, just know this:

I was accepted to both Cornell and Columbia, but flat out rejected from schools that aren't in the top 100 *US News* rankings.

How is that possible? How was I accepted to two such highly ranked colleges, yet rejected from others with such low rankings? The reason is simple: *college applications are always a crapshoot.* The same kid can get accepted to Harvard and rejected from Yale. Into Duke and booted from Vanderbilt. Accepted to Amherst and rejected from Williams. There's not some objective point at which you're "good enough for schools above X ranking." This is a *subjective process.* Depending on the mood of an admissions officer, or the precise things that a particular school is looking for that year, you might be a perfect fit, or an immediate rejection. Plan accordingly.

If you have a 95% chance of getting in somewhere, it's *not* the same thing as being *guaranteed* to get in. **You MUST have a backup plan - and you MUST be sure that your "backup plan" is actually a plan that you're thrilled with.**

In other words, don't think of your "safety schools" as "horrible places where you'll end up if you fail." Think of them the right way: as "lower-ranked, yet still awesome, universities where I'll be able to grow as a person and enhance my mind."

If you have one particular "dream school," that's fantastic. Go for it. But do not *ever* hinge your entire college journey on that one school - it's unrealistic and counterproductive.

This book will teach you to pick a wide variety of *awesome* schools that you're *thrilled* to apply to, so that, no matter where you get in, you'll be able to become a vastly more awesome person.

As long as we're on the same page, we can move on.

CHAPTER 4

Who the Heck Am I?

U sually, books *end* with an "about the author" section. But advice is only as good as its source. With that in mind, I want to quickly share my background in the field, which might shed some light on why I wrote this book, and why I hope you'll listen to the advice within.

I'm not a childhood psychologist. I'm not a parent. I don't have a degree in education, and I don't have a PhD in developmental science. I was never on the admissions committee of any college, and I'm not a certified college consultant. I'm also very young. So who am I to write this thing?

I'm someone with over 15,000 hours of real, hands-on experience in the college admissions industry. As a career SAT and ACT tutor, I've worked with over 400 students one-on-one, and observed the results of the *thousands more* who've worked through my online program. I've helped to craft the applications and essays of hundreds of students, worked alongside some of the best college consultants in the world, and seen *exactly* what *does* and *doesn't* work in every single case. My position and experiences have allowed me to receive *direct, instant feedback,* watching the triumphs and failures of the most competitive applicants in the world.

Put simply: I don't like sharing theories. I like sharing *facts.* Every word in this book is based on my extensive, real-life, hands-on experience. Zero conjecture included.

I would argue that there are few other people on Earth who've had as much experience observing students' entire college application process, from start to finish, and figuring out what does and doesn't work. If you're looking for a "creative" approach to college applications, or a "new age" solution to the educational scenario in this country, look elsewhere. But if you want a simple, honest account of exactly how this all works, read on.

This is the book I've wanted to write for years, and that I feel every family with a college-bound student needs to read. Every line in this book is based on countless real-world experiences. Ignore the advice within at your own peril - follow it and make your life much easier.

Three Quick Notes:

1. **This book is meant for both parents and students, but the entire thing is written in the second person.** If I say that "you need to get better grades," and you're a parent, it means that *you need to make sure your kid gets better grades.* The distinctions are obvious – and I'll make it clear if I'm speaking specifically to parents or students throughout the book. Speaking of which:
2. **If you're a parent, send this book to your kid. If you're a student, send this book to your parent(s).** You all need to be on the same page – it'll make life a thousand times easier.
3. **To avoid ponderous sentence structure, I'll use the pronoun "he" to refer to all singular subjects.** This is not to show a preference for one sex or another, but simply to simplify the horrendous "he or she" grammar construct that plagues so many books. If you're a female student, or have a daughter – I'm talking to you, too!

Section Two: The Map

It's tough to travel when you have no idea where you are or where you're going.

CHAPTER 5

Set Your Targets Correctly (Being Your College's "Type")

T he college application process is a journey. And you'll never embark on a successful journey if you have no idea where you're trying to go.

While everyone wants to go to a "good college," few families have a **properly developed list of colleges, and even fewer have defined what "good" actually means *for them**. They know that they want to go to "the best school possible," and they might have a few names loosely floating on a list, but that's simply not enough.

I know what you're probably thinking:

"Yeah, yeah - I know, picking a good college is important...*but what do I do to get in!"*

In case you think I'm beating around the bush, I want to make something clear.

The next few sections of this book are all about the strategies and tactics necessary to gain admission to the schools that you choose. And if you're dying to get to them, you can skip ahead – just know that doing so would be an enormous mistake. First, pick the right colleges – *then* learn how to get into them. Failing to approach the process in this order is disastrous. Why?

Arguably THE most important step you can take to *get into* the right colleges is *applying to the right colleges in the first place!*

The dating analogy rears its ugly head once again. Imagine that you're interested in dating a certain girl, but she's absolutely *crazy* for *guitarists* with *tattoos*. You don't play the guitar, and you don't have any tattoos - but *come on - you're just such a good guy! Of course you can still win her heart!*

Nope. You just weren't her *type.* It doesn't matter how handsome or funny or kind you are - if she *demands* a guitarist with tattoos, and you don't fit the bill, it's just not going to happen.

Colleges all have a "type" as well - and if you're not the "type" that a college is looking for, there's no point in applying. Conversely, if you're the exact "type" for a certain college, you'll get in *much* more easily.

We've all seen it before: some guy is dating some girl, and we simply *can't believe* that he went for her (or vice versa). But for whatever reason, they both float each other's boats. It goes without saying that the colleges you pick should float *your* boat, but you need to float *their boats*, too.

College applications simply don't work *unless you're attracted to <u>each other.</u>* Let's take a look at both sides of that coin.

You Better Be "Into It"

If I had a dollar for every time a family told me that they were applying to a school "because they heard it was decent," or because "it has a pretty good reputation," I'd be a millionaire. Unfortunately, this is as horrendous as it is commonplace.

Do not EVER spend four years of your life at the wrong college simply because you're too lazy to do your research!

If your idea of "research" is looking at rankings and picking the highest ones, you have some work to do.

If you've refined your list by weeding out the schools that aren't in "states you like" or that "aren't in big cities," you've still got *a long way to go.*

Imagine a friend telling you that he's getting married in five months. Excited, you say, "Wow, congrats! How'd you meet her? Tell me all about her!"

He responds: "Actually, we haven't met yet, and I don't really know anything about her at all. But she was on a list of "people who were good to date," and that sounded pretty cool to me, so I mean, I'm just gonna go for it."

Sound ridiculous? That's because it *is* ridiculous - and applying to colleges without doing thorough research is *just as ridiculous – if not more so*. **You NEED to spend the time researching EVERYTHING about the schools to which you want to apply - both the ones already on your radar *and* the ones you might not even know about yet!**

Hopefully I've made my point. Yet there's one more reason why picking the right schools is so insanely important: **motivation.**

Proper Motivation is the Secret Sauce

Want to know how to accomplish something amazing? *Be really, really into it.*

Without motivation, nothing remarkable is possible. With motivation, anything is possible. That's why I always find it so amusing when parents try to "force" their kids to play baseball or football or chess, as if external motivation could create an all-star athlete or chess master. No such luck. The kids who end up as amazing basketball players are the kids who you *can't keep off the court*, and the kids who end up as chess masters are the ones who you catch in bed playing chess at 4am under their blankets with a flashlight.

If you aren't *motivated* to get into college, then every part of your college application will be lackluster. And the best way to get motivated by the college process is to *see yourself at the EXACT schools you're applying to.*

Doing the proper research can take some time, but it is *incredibly* motivating. Whenever I meet an unmotivated student, the reason is almost always the same: he has no idea why he actually wants to go to college.

"Yeah - my mom picked a few schools for me, and then I heard that U Chicago was sort of cool, so I mean. Yeah. That's where I want to go, I guess?"

What? You say he's not *burning with desire* to work on his applications? What are the chances?!

If you want to get into an awesome school, *get motivated.* Schools can smell motivation (and lack thereof) from *miles away.* When you're truly motivated, getting good grades and test scores, wowing your teachers, rocking interviews, and putting together an amazing extracurricular profile is easy. Without motivation, you'll end up half-heartedly doing everything you do - and admissions officers will take note.

There's nothing more motivating than *finding the perfect school,* learning everything about it, and then setting your sights upon it. Most students are motivated in two ways, both of which are incredibly ineffective:

1. *Externally* by their parents, which looks like this:
   "Do all your homework, or else...."
   "If you do this, I'll be happy."
   "If you don't get into Harvard, your father and I will be so angry..."
   "If you don't finish your homework, you're grounded."
2. *Vaguely,* like this:
   "I think that college should be more fun than high school."
   "Doesn't a good college get you more money?"
   "College looks awesome in movies."
   "I want to go to college in a city - cities are great."

The problem is that **external and vague motivations are about 5% as effective as SPECIFIC, INTERNAL motivation**. When you know *exactly* what *you* want, what it looks like, why you want it, and how to get it, you'll do everything possible to achieve your goal. If other people are telling you what you're supposed to want, or if you don't know what you really want at all, then you won't do jack.

The one true key to college success is to develop a hyper-specific list of colleges that provide you with exactly the kinds of opportunities you want in life.

Once you've found these schools, the rest of your work is practically done for you. Studying for the SAT or ACT, working on that chemistry project, and spending some extra time at soccer practice are all much easier when you know *why* you're going through the process. Without a clear picture of your goal in mind, it all seems like busywork. With a clear, internalized goal, it's easy as pie.

With that in mind, I'll show you exactly how to pick the schools that not only *work for you*, but that *want you to attend as well.* From there, things get easier and easier.

CHAPTER 6

How to Pick the Schools You Really Want (and That Really Want You)

As I mentioned in the last chapter, nothing stinks quite like lack of motivation. Applying to a college that you're not actually into is like checking your emails during a date - a bit transparent, to say the least. And if there's one thing that college admissions officers are trained to sniff out, it's **an applicant who doesn't actually want to be there.**

<u>The easiest way to get rejected from *any* college is to make it clear that you're not going to go if they let you in.</u>

We'll cover this concept in much more depth later on. For now, just remember these three facts:

1. **Colleges care about their reputations more than almost anything else in the world.**
2. **A college's reputation is dependent largely upon its ranking.**
3. **A college's ranking is largely dependent upon <u>the percentage of admitted applicants who actually attend</u>.**

Harvard isn't just Harvard because it lets in so few of its applicants - there are actually plenty of colleges with lower admission percentages. Harvard is Harvard because *practically everyone who gets into Harvard ends up going.*

The admissions officers at Harvard know that if they let you in, you're probably going to show up. The less competitive the school, the less assured the admissions officers become. Yet, even at the most competitive schools in the world, a "crappy cover letter" is a surefire way to get the boot.

What do I mean by "a crappy cover letter?" When I was running my tutoring firm, I'd get a ton of resumes from aspiring tutors with cover letters that looked like this:

> *"I want to work at your firm because it is excellent, and because I think it is a place where I will learn a lot and also have valuable work experience. You have a good reputation, and I think it will be a good opportunity to work there. Your firm is a place where I will be able to show my talents."*

That cover letter was obviously sent to at least twenty different tutoring firms. It said *nothing* about my firm, but it said *plenty* about the applicant. He was *too lazy to do his research*, he was *happy with any outcome*, and *he had low standards for himself and his own work*. Pathetic. The second I saw a letter like that, it was over.

Here's the college application version:

Q: Why do you want to attend Harvard University?
A: I want to attend your university because it is a well-ranked school with a fine reputation and amazing academic programs. The teachers, in particular, are quite good, and also, you have extracurricular activities that I'm very excited to be a part of. The location is also amazing, as I will be able to explore the culture of your community with all my might, and also, I will be able to contribute much to the community while I am there.

See the big issue here? This answer could apply to *any college in the universe!* Whoever wrote this sort of answer obviously hasn't done a lick of homework on Harvard, what it's all about, and what it has to offer. Therefore, you can be *sure* that he has no idea what he can offer Harvard, either. (See the bigger problem starting to emerge?)

If you can't convince a school that you *actually* want to go there, and that you'll attend if accepted, you raise a red flag - you let the admissions officers know that you're probably going to *damage* their reputation by *not* attending. This is *not* what they want to see.

But it gets worse.

Even if you *do* end up attending, you don't know anything about the school - so what are you going to do when you end up there?

Remember: colleges want students who can *give them something*. So what will you contribute *while you attend*? That's the second part of the puzzle, and the biggest problem with a crappy cover letter. If you don't know anything about the colleges to which you're applying, you make it glaringly obvious that you have no real idea what you'll contribute once you get in. Therefore, admissions officers assume the worst: you'll drink, mess around, and "hang out," without really contributing much of anything.

Compare the crappy cover letter above to that of a student who has actually done the research, learned about the school, and figured out precisely why he's dying to attend:

Q: Why do you want to attend Columbia University?
A: My entire life, I've been enamored with the concept of comedy writing. Columbia offers countless opportunities to both improve my writing skills and contribute my writing while I'm there. Your creative writing program is world-famous for producing talented writers, especially in the comedy space, and professors X and Y have been personal heroes of mine for years - I'd love the opportunity to spend even five minutes learning from them! As I continue honing my skills, I want to contribute to the many comedy publications available through the school - the Jester in particular. I'm already a subscriber, and I can't wait for the opportunity to offer articles and cartoons (if they'll have me). Finally, Columbia is near some of the best comedy clubs in New York City, which will give me an opportunity to hone my craft. I have a few friends who are currently attending Columbia, and they're all members of the comedy club - another huge reason why I'm dying to go! I'm joining the *second* I enroll.

Anyone from the Columbia admissions committee who read this would quickly see three things:

1. This student has clearly done his research - he's talking about *Columbia*, and not some generic school.

2.   This student really, really wants to go to Columbia - if he gets in, he's there.
3.   This student will *do stuff while he's at Columbia!* He'll write for the paper. He'll participate in clubs. He'll actively participate in his classes. He'll *make Columbia a better school.*

All three are essential.

As I'll remind you countless times throughout this book, **you need to offer colleges something if you want to get in**. If you don't, they'll kick your application to the curb. **In order to offer colleges something, you need to know about those specific colleges!** If you don't, how will you ever learn what they want, and what you have to offer?

So how do you "fool" a college into thinking you actually want to go, and that you've researched it thoroughly? **_You don't._** Believe it or not, you actually have to want to go, and you actually have to do your research! And lest you think that I'm just saying this for purely philosophical/moral reasons, know something else:

Admissions officers are *unbelievably good* at picking up on *rubbish*.

They have literally seen it all. They've read *thousands upon thousands* of applications. They know what a sincere, honestly researched, enthusiastic application looks like, they know what a lukewarm application looks like, and they know what a totally full of rubbish, insincere application looks like. There is no fooling them.

You have to do your research - no ifs, ands, or buts about it. You need to want to go to the colleges you're applying to, and you need to pick the colleges that are looking for *you* and *your type of personality, profile, and attribute set.*

How do you find the right schools?
This is the easy part. Here's the entire process:

1.   **Figure out EXACTLY what you want to *get out of* your college experience.**
2.   **Figure out EXACTLY what you can *provide to* your college.**

3. **Find colleges that'll give you what you want, and that want what you're trying to give.**

The first two steps don't even require any research. They just require some soul-searching. Let's take a closer look at each:

1. **What are you trying to get from the college that you attend?**
   You will be spending four years of your life here. Make them count. The only answers that *aren't* allowed are "a degree" and "telling people that I went there." Everything else works. Here are some examples:

   - The best [subject of your choice] teachers in the world
   - A wide variety of intramural clubs and teams
   - An amazing newspaper that'll allow you to practice your skills as a journalist
   - A feeling of community
   - A world-class coach in your particular sport
   - Incredible science resources to help you further your research
   - A cutting-edge entrepreneurship program to help you develop your skills as a businessperson
   - Integrated vocational training to help you earn work skills as you focus on your academics
   - In incredible internship program that puts you in touch with [industry X, Y, or Z]
   - A campus rich in architectural history / natural beauty
   - Extremely hands-on faculty advisors who can help you to pick classes and guide your academic decisions
   - Small classes with intimate discussions
   - Large lectures headlined by world-famous speakers
   - An integrated medical / business / legal curriculum
   - The ability to take graduate school classes while getting your undergraduate degree
   - A location in the middle of a booming metropolis / in the middle of nature / somewhere in between
   - The ability to work while you attend so that you can earn some money and pay down your student loans
   - A library full of rare books on [topic of your choice]

These answers can be as broad or as specific as possible. But you need a long, thorough list. If you skimp on this list, you're just screwing yourself.

If you can't figure out the reasons why you want to go to college, why are you even applying?

Before you move on, make a list of at least 15 items, and then rank them in order of importance. Use that list to *craft your dream school*. Once you know exactly what you want, you'll easily be able to find the schools that can give it to you.

Notice, by the way, that none of this has anything to do with ranking. You should be focusing on the qualities of the schools themselves, and *not* on where they stand on some list. You need to get excited and motivated to attend, and you'll only get excited if they *offer you what you want out of life*. Nothing else matters.

Once you have that taken care of, you should move to the next step:

2. **What are you offering to whichever school you end up attending?**
    In later chapters, we'll explore this question in much more depth, and figure out how to properly present your gifts to admissions officers. For now, just make a list of *everything* that you bring to the table, and then stack these gifts in order of importance. Are you bringing:

    -   Active engagement and participation in all your classes?
    -   Writing skills that can be used in university publications?
    -   Community-building and leadership skills that can be used to form, organize, and lead clubs and organizations throughout campus?
    -   Philanthropic passion that you can use to help the surrounding community and better the name of the college?
    -   Creative thinking skills that'll allow you to improve the school's campus/classes/offerings/clubs/policies/etc.?
    -   Leadership skills that'll allow you to take an active, effective, and constructive role in campus politics?
    -   Incredible athletic ability that'll help to improve one of the school's sports teams?
    -   Incredible musical ability that'll help to improve the bands, orchestras, etc., on campus?

- The ability to raise funds and build passion for a cause, which could be used to help the school raise money from and throw events for alumni?
- Incredible artistic ability that'll add to school galleries, enhance school art programs, and more?

What is your secret sauce? What's in it for THEM?

Don't be shy here. Think of everything. Just make sure that it's *authentic* and *truly you*. Saying that you're bringing your philanthropy to the table because you gave blood one time last year doesn't count. List everything, and then order it from most to the least important (and if you're not sure what counts as "most important," don't worry - we'll be getting into that in much more detail later on - for now, just focus on the stuff that's *most obviously legitimate*).

Once you've done all that, it's time to move on to the most important step:

3. **Find colleges that will both *give you what you want* and that are *looking for what you have to give*. Don't stop until you have a list of TWENTY.** As you might have suspected, this is the most complicated step of them all - and it takes the most work. That's also why it's the most important. An in-depth knowledge of each college is extremely important here, and short-cuts won't really work.

   There are many ways to go about this, so I'll list them all in no particular order. Choose the ones you want to roll with, and then *act on them*. It's never too early to start this process. And by the way: I'm not saying you can't use *US News and World Report*'s ranking system to match the qualities that you find appealing with some top-notch schools. I'm just saying that you should *start* with school qualities, and *then* correlate them with rankings. Going by ranking alone is an absolutely terrible idea.

Here are some ways to find the right schools:

A) **Your school's college advisor.**
   This is a free, readily available, and usually reliable source. If there's one thing that your college advisor brings to the table, it's his *extremely*

in-depth knowledge of the particular qualities of colleges across the country (and the world). He might know about particular schools that are *exact* matches that you might not have considered. He might also know which schools absolutely *aren't* looking for a student like you. In any event, this is the first place you should go. If you already have an advisor, set up an appointment ASAP. If not, see if you can get an appointment as soon as possible.

B) An independent college consultant.
If you have the means, I highly recommend working with a certified, independent college advisor. While some are better than others, most certified private college advisors have encyclopedic knowledge of the nation's schools. Their knowledge combined with your lists will lead to a very productive discussion. If you want to find a consultant in your area, you can check out the Independent Educational Consultants Association website here:

http://www.iecaonline.com/cfm_PublicSearch/pg_PublicSearch. cfm?mode=entry

Don't work with anyone who isn't certified.

Just be aware that while they're worth every penny, they usually aren't cheap.

A few other things to note before working with *any* independent consultant:

-   Make sure to look up reviews online.
-   Make sure to speak with at least two past clients to check legitimacy.
-   Above all else, be sure to look for *results*. Anyone can make claims about how good they are, but the proof is in the pudding. Find out how many of their clients are going to their top-choice schools, and figure out which schools their clients are getting into. You can't fake reality

C) CollegeData.com : http://www.collegedata.com
College Data has an *insane* amount of information on every college in the world. You can use this site to figure out which colleges have which qualities,

ranging from academic opportunities and scholarship programs to sports competition levels and location.

Take a look whenever you have a chance. You'll be blown away.

D) **College "Discovery" Books.**

Leafing through these can take a bit of time, but you'll find some real gems if you're willing to put in the effort. A few of my absolute favorites:

The Fiske Guide to Colleges

The Ultimate Guide to America's Best Colleges

Colleges That Change Lives

The Best 380 Colleges

America's Best Colleges for B Students

The Best Value Colleges

If you can't find twenty colleges you like using these books, you have some pretty unrealistic standards!

E) **The College Board portal:**
https://bigfuture.collegeboard.org/college-search

The College Board has put together a pretty nifty tool here. Use it to search for colleges by majors offered, activities offered, campus setups, etc.

As you go through this process, just remember the two fundamentals:

1. **You need to find colleges that you actually want to attend.**

The real key is to focus on colleges that *provide you with ways to further your life goals.* Start to implant the idea of "the dream school" into your mind. Realize that schools *can be* places where you can chase your dreams, broaden your horizons, and turn into the person who you want to be - *but only if you pick the right schools!* Once you find something you like, get as much information as you can - pamphlets, brochures, websites, statistics, pictures, student testimonials, descriptions of programs, etc., and tear through them. Once you have a solid idea of where you really want to spend time, motivation takes care of itself. Spend a week fantasizing about the places where you'll be spending the next four years of your life. Once you're *burning* to get into a particular college, 90% of your work is done. Then comes step two:

2. **You need to find colleges that actually want *you* to attend.**

   Most of the remainder of this book is dedicated to *figuring out precisely how this works* and *making your application as appealing as possible*. However, if you arrange discussions with your advisors, read the right books and websites, and do some good old-fashioned research, you'll be way ahead of the game.

   For instance, RISD doesn't want kids who're trying to become stockbrokers. Cal Tech isn't looking for novelists. If you have a 1.9 GPA, you're not going to Harvard. If a school doesn't have a crew team, you're not getting recruited for crew. All of this might seem somewhat obvious, but *you'd be surprised...*

   As we keep moving through this book, we'll further refine this process. For now, just *develop your list* and *wrap your mind around it*. You can't make progress until you figure out where you're trying to go.

   Feel free to read to the end of this book and soak up all the information before you go through all these steps. But once you're done, flip back to this chapter and go through every one of my instructions step by step. This isn't something to be *read* - it's something to be *done*.

CHAPTER 7

Start Your Visitation and Research Plan NOW

Now that you've put together your initial list, it's time to refine and improve it. The twenty schools on your list aren't necessarily the twenty that you'll apply to (and don't worry - you won't have to apply to twenty schools!). But this list will serve as your foundation - from here, you can take schools away, add new ones on, and enhance your chances of getting into all of them.

Building on Your Foundation

Now you know where you're trying to go. This is where the process *really* begins. I've put this chapter this early on in the book because it's the element of your application process that requires the most planning, time, and advance effort. *Waiting until the last minute to research and visit your schools a huge mistake.* You have to start *now*.

There are a few things you need to do with every school on your list if you want to maximize your chances of both getting in and ending up at a place that'll make you happy. They are, in order of effort and time required (from most to least):

1. **Visiting the campus.**
2. **Arranging an interview.**
3. **Creating a full college profile**
4. **"Slotting" yourself into the college's framework**

All of these steps are important. As with most things in life, the most challenging and time-consuming ones are also the *most* important. Here's how to handle all of them:

Arranging Campus Visits

There's no substitute for visiting a college's campus. No matter how many pictures you look at or student reviews you read, you'll never get the "feel" for a place unless you're actually there.

Without trashing any schools, I'll just say this: my original top choice college was *not* my top choice after I visited its campus. I absolutely hated it there. Once I actually walked around, saw the (miserable) student body, got a feel for the musty, horrific buildings and stifled atmosphere, I never wanted to go there again. If I hadn't visited, I never would have known this - and I might have ended up somewhere absolutely awful.

More than simply eliminating possibilities from your list, visits provide *serious* inspiration. It's one thing to look at a school's brochure - it's another thing to actually be on campus, breathe the air, and really *see yourself there*. If you want to get pumped up on this process, campus visits are *the* way to do it.

Aside from helping you to select (and cull) the schools on your list, and to provide enhanced motivation, campus visits do something else very important: *they allow you to demonstrate your interest in the schools by getting your visit on record AND by doing **advanced research for your applications and supplementary essays**.*

As you already know, colleges *need* to know that you'll show up if they let you in. Submitting a "crappy cover letter" is a surefire way to get rejected. If you actually show up on campus, and make it clear that you've been there, you're *automatically bypassing this concern*.

When you go on your visits, it's essential that you conduct **advanced research.** Do *everything you possibly can* to learn about the school, its campus, its history, its classes, its activities, its facilities and resources, its teachers, it dorms - *everything*. The more you learn, the more excited you'll get, and the more detailed your supplementary essays will become. These are all very good things.

How to Arrange Campus Visits

Just Google "visit / tour [school]," go to the school's website, and check out their tour schedule.

Most schools offer campus tours year-round. Others even let you stay overnight at dorms to get a true feel for the student experience! It all depends on the school, but a simple Google search will let you know.

If you're looking at all local colleges, this process is pretty simple and inexpensive. If you're looking at colleges all around the country (or the world), it's obviously much more expensive and time-consuming.

If you don't have the time or resources to jet around the country and check out every school on your list, it's not the end of the world - just know that you're not applying to an actual college - you're applying to *the idea of a college*, which can be a bit misleading. Try as hard as you can to get to every college on your list, but don't fret if you can't.

As you'll quickly realize, there's a reason why I want you thinking about this *now*, not later - visiting just one college can take an entire weekend. Get out your calendar and get to work - this takes time.

To kill two birds with one stone, you'll also want to set up an interview while you're on campus:

Arranging Your Interview

There are few colleges in the world that *require* an interview. Some colleges maintain that they don't use the interview *in any way* during their evaluation process, whether you bomb it or ace it. Others take your interview quite seriously, but don't hold it against you if you don't interview (or so they say…).

Do you *need* to interview? No. But you *should* interview whenever possible. We'll get into *how* to do this later. For now, just know that an interview is one of the best ways to show your true interest in a school, and to let your personality shine through. Without your interview, it's easy for you to be "a number" - just a binder sitting on some admission officer's desk. With an interview, you become a living, breathing human being.

Your interview is also an amazing way to learn more about the schools you're visiting. One of the best tips for a great interview is to *show active interest in the school* and *ask a lot of specific, research-driven questions*. Don't ask stuff that you can find out on any brochure (how many students are there? how many times has your football team won the division title? Etc.). Ask stuff that you can't find out from the brochure, and that shows the level of attention that you're paying to the school. The interviewer will take note, and you'll get even more amped on attending.

If you take the time to arrange a college visit, then you absolutely *must* arrange an interview while you're there (if possible).

How do you figure out how to do this? Google!

Just type in "[School X] interview policy" and "get an interview at [school x]," check out the school's official website, and figure out how it works. Every school is different, so this is something that you'll need to find out for yourself. Just know that if you *can* do an interview, you should.

What if you're not able to visit campus? Can you still get an interview? Absolutely! A lot of colleges offer "satellite interviews." For instance, I had my Columbia interview at a law firm office in downtown Boston. How do you set *these* up? You guessed it - Google! Just type "off-campus interview [school x]" and see what comes up.

Again, we'll be covering a few tips to ace your interviews later on. For now, just figure out if and when you can make them happen.

Creating a Full College Profile

Once you've developed your list of colleges, you'll want to dig deeper. Just because a college sounds great at first glance doesn't mean that it's somewhere you'll want to end up, or somewhere that wants your "type."

How do you learn more? I'm about to *blow your mind*: GOOGLE!

Check each school's website. Read reviews. Read criticisms. Look at pictures and videos of the campus. Learn more about the extracurriculars. Find out how much the average graduate earns. Learn more about job placement statistics. See which majors and minors they offer, and which are the most and least lucrative for graduates. There's a lot more out there than the simple descriptions in guidebooks.

You can never do too much research.

Keep a binder, online folder, or Google Docs page for each college and take extensive notes. Figure out where you *really* want to end up, where you *kind of* want to end up, and which colleges you can scratch off your list.

Once you get a full, accurate picture of each school, it's time to figure out whether you can get in.

"Slotting Yourself"

Want to know the best way to figure out your chances of getting into a school? Metrics.

As you'll learn shortly, the "chopping block process" for most schools follows this pattern:

1. Does the student have some sort of "red carpet voucher" (i.e. athletic recruitment, enormous donation, etc.) that allows him to bypass the regular admissions process? If so, move him to step three or four. If not, go to step two.
2. Are the student's grades and test scores good enough? If not, chop him! If so, move to step three.
3. Does the student have anything remarkable to offer to this school? If not - chop him! If so, move to step four:
4. Admission!

This is a blatant simplification, but for the time being, you just need to get a general idea of where you do and don't stand a chance. The first step in this process is to get an idea of a school's *metrics*. Doing so is easy:

1. Go to Google
2. Type in "SAT scores [School X]"
3. Click on the CollegeApps.About.com link for that school (it'll usually be the first or second result)
4. Read about the school's metrics

Here's an example of Harvard's About.com profile:

http://collegeapps.about.com/od/collegeprofiles/p/harvard_profile.htm

From within, you can check out an "SAT/ACT and GPA map" to get an idea of the GPA and test score combinations that get accepted and rejected, and use the cappex. com tool to calculate your chances of getting in. Of course, this number is somewhat meaningless (what does a 37% chance of getting into a school actually mean?) - but it'll give you a general idea of where you stand.

We're going to get *much* more scientific about this later on, but for now, just do the following:

1. Figure out whether your GPA is lower, higher, or on par with the average GPA accepted by the school.
2. Do the same with your SAT/ACT scores. (If you don't have any yet, or they need to be raised, don't worry - I'll show you how to take care of that later on.) If you're *on par* with the school's GPA and SAT/ACT requirements, it's a *maybe*. If you're well *above* these numbers, it's a *safety*. And if you're below these requirements, it's a *reach*. If you're *well* below these requirements, it's a "no way in heck," unless you have some sort of red carpet application (recruited athlete, enormous donor, etc.).
3. Segregate your schools by category. You should have an equal number of reaches, maybes, and safeties.

Also, take a moment to look at each school's mission statement (which is also printed in the About.com page for each school). Is it in line with your goals? Does it sound like the school is looking for someone like you? Just get a general idea - we'll be visiting this question in much more depth shortly.

Finito!

That's all there is to it! Now that you have your list out of the way, and you have a plan for researching, refining, and enhancing the list, it's time to figure out *what needs to get done before you apply*. First, we'll look at the big picture. Then we'll get into the nitty gritty.

CHAPTER 8

Plan EVERYTHING In Advance (Plus the Ultimate Application Checklist/Calendar)

There's *a lot* to do if you want to get into the best colleges in the country. Sticking your head in the sand and ignoring it isn't a strategy. Instead, I want you to see it as a whole, confront it, and then figure out exactly *when* you're going to tackle it.

The rest of this book will be focused on the "*how to*" of each of these elements. For now, I just want you to know the *whats* and the *whens*.

Below, you'll find **My Ultimate Application Checklist and Calendar**, which will show you every single thing you need to accomplish during this process and when it needs to get done. If you don't know what some of this stuff is, or if you have questions about it, don't worry - all will be explained by the end of this book.

Take a look to get an idea of the entire process and timeline. Bookmark or print these pages (and share them with your friends so they're not left in the dust!). Once you're done, we'll get into the fun stuff.

The Ultimate College Application Checklist:

Before the Application Begins:

☐ Maintain high grades - a bad freshman year still weighs down your GPA
    ↑ Start: Freshman Fall

☐ Cut all classes which unnecessarily drag down your GPA
    ↑ Start: Freshman Fall. Continue indefinitely.

☐ Figure out your "one thing"
    ↑ Start: Freshman Fall. Continue indefinitely.

☐ Learn speed reading as soon as possible
    ↑ Start: Freshman Fall

☐ Research your list of reach, "maybe," and "safety" schools
    ↑ Start: Freshman Fall. Continue indefinitely.

☐ Arrange campus visits to as many schools as possible
    ↑ Start: Freshman Fall.
Continue until all schools have been visited.

☐ Arrange on-site interviews with as many schools as possible.
    ↑ Coincides with visits.

☐ Arrange off-site interviews with the rest.
    ↑ Start: as soon as your list is created.

☐ Figure out, as early as possible, whether to take the SAT or ACT
    ↑ Start: freshman year (or now, if it's later than freshman year)

☐ If necessary, get learning disability and other special accommodations as soon as possible for the SAT and/or ACT
    ↑ Start: Freshman year

☐ Find out the subject test requirements of all your target schools
    ↑ Start: As soon as you have your list

☐ If desired/necessary, research any test-optional schools
    ↑ Start: As soon as you have your list

☐ Figure out if and when you plan on taking AP classes / exams
    ↑ Start: As soon as academic trends develop.
Don't take any that you aren't confident you'll be able to master.

☐ Undergo a full SAT/ACT prep program until your scores on practice tests are in the 25-75 range of the schools to which you're applying
    ↑ Start:Freshman year, or as soon as possible if freshman year is over
Continue until target scores attained

☐ Take your SAT/ACT
     ↑ Start/Finish: when your scores
       are at the desired level.

☐ Figure out which SAT Subject Tests you'll be taking
     ↑ Start: Beginning of freshman year.

☐ Take all your SAT Subject Tests
     ↑ Finished: when all required tests for all target
colleges have been completed and you've achieved high scores

☐ Request your recommendation letters
     ↑ Start: End of junior year.

☐ Start planning your essay(s)
     ↑ Start: End of junior year.

☐ If you're getting recruited, reach out to recruiting agents as soon as possible.
     ↑ Start: Summer after freshman year
(or whenever impressive times/performances have been produced)

☐ If you're getting recruited, secure a letter of intent
     ↑ Start: As early as possible,
but no later than the summer after junior year.

☐ Finalize your list of colleges with your school or independent counselor
     ↑ Finish by the end of the summer after junior year,
or within a week or two of senior fall.

Preparing and Submitting Your Application:

☐ Download copies or make online accounts for all applications
     ↑ Summer before senior year

☐ Figure out the regular and early application deadlines for all schools in question
     ↑ Summer before senior year

☐ Decide whether you'll apply Early Decision or Early Action (and to which school(s))
     ↑ Summer before senior year

☐ Request that your high school transcript be sent to all schools to which you're applying
  ↑ Senior Fall (or by application deadlines)

☐ If necessary, request a mid-year grade report sent to all schools to which you're applying
  ↑ If you're deferred from Early Decision/Action, or if you're applying regular

☐ Send all SAT, ACT, SAT Subject Tests, AP, and all other scores required or desired by each school
  ↑ Craft all accounts by senior fall, send before application deadlines

☐ Finalize your essay(s)
  ↑ Summer before senior year, or senior fall at the latest

☐ Submit your essay(s)
  ↑ At time of application

☐ Write and send your supplemental essays for each school
  ↑ Summer before senior year. Send along with your application(s)

☐ Politely remind your teachers of recommendation deadlines. Secure recommendations well before application deadlines
  ↑ Senior fall

☐ Complete your actual application
  ↑ At least a week before deadline(s)

☐ Get fee waivers for your application(s) (if necessary)
  ↑ Summer before senior year

☐ Submit your actual application(s)
  ↑ Senior fall (by application deadlines)

☐ Make copies of and get confirmation of all applications and application materials
  ↑ Make copies before application, get confirmation(s) immediately after submitting

☐ If necessary, send additional materials
  ↑ After applications are sent (as soon as possible)

☐ If necessary, submit FAFSA, PROFILE, college aid form, and state aid form
  ↑ By deadlines (have arranged by summer before senior year)

Once You're Done:

☐ Meet the deadline to accept your admission
   ↑ Upon early Decision acceptance (if ED)
   ↑ By senior spring (if EA or regular)

☐ Send your deposit to the college of your choice
   ↑ By the deposit deadline - senior spring

☐ Accept financial aid offer (If Necessary)
   ↑ By the deadline - senior spring

☐ Notify all other colleges that accepted you that you will not be attending
   ↑ Immediately after notifying college you're attending

☐ Write thank you notes to all the teachers who recommended you
   ↑ Before the end of senior year

☐ Send the author of this book a present. He's probably particularly fond of bulldog puppies and/or rare editions of old books
   ↑ Immediately

Section Three: Fundamentals

Or: How to get your act together and take care of the most important things first

CHAPTER 9

The Two Things That Actually Matter (and the one exception)

Quick note: every admissions committee is slightly different, and the process I'm about to describe here varies a bit from school to school, but, for the vast majority of schools, the vast majority of the time, this is how it works.

When admissions officers view your application, they use a *hierarchy*. Some things matter more than others. Not only do they matter *more* than others, but they also matter *before* others.

To understand this chapter, and the admissions process as a whole, I want you to put yourself in the shoes of a college admissions officer. She has countless applications to review, she's under enormous time pressure, and she realizes that both her college's reputation *and* the fates and emotions of thousands of fragile high school students are on the line. It's not an easy job.

Like all people, she strives to make her job both *easier* and *more effective*. And if the school she works for is like the vast majority of other schools, systems are available to help her do both.

You should imagine the application review process happening in three stages. Here they are:

1. **Red Carpet Applications**
2. **Shallow Metrics**
3. **You**

Schools don't spend time thoroughly reviewing every single application. To do so would be ludicrous. They've safeguarded themselves *somewhat* from frivolous applications by tacking on a fee and supplementary essays, but I emphasize the word *somewhat* for a reason. If I had a dollar for every time an unqualified student applied to Ivies "just to see what happens," I'd be eating lobster on my yacht right now.

To save time (and sanity), admissions officers work through three distinct stages. By the end of this book, you'll have an extremely thorough idea of how all three stages work. But first, you need to understand the basics:

Red Carpet Applications

A "red carpet application" is basically any application *personally backed by someone of importance to the university's reputational or financial construct.* What do I mean by a "personally backed?" I mean that they've let the admissions officers know, either in person or by means of a marking system, that your application *must* be considered, and favorably.

These applications, of course, get sorted to the top of the pile. Once you have a red carpet voucher on your side, it's pretty tough to get rejected.

How do you know if you have a voucher on your side? *If you have to ask, you don't.*

Some of the things you'll get a voucher for:

- **Your grandfather donated a wing of the library.**

Quick note: there are people out there who claim that enormous donations don't sway admissions officers. To which I say: * cue uproarious laughter *

True, the *size* of sway-worthy donations is much more intimidating now (you're not getting into a reach school for $6,000 - that's not even a term's tuition), but if you're donating millions, it's still a big deal.

- **You're a recruited athlete.** A lot of people point out how ridiculous it is that recruited athletes have such an unfair advantage in the college process. I'd say that they're right. I was a recruited rower, and I still think this system is BS. But it's the way it is.
- **You're a "celebrity,"** which used loosely, means that *just by attending, you will raise the status of the school due purely to your awesomeness.* Not sure if you're a celebrity or not? You're not.
- **In *some* cases, your parents/relatives are alumni.**
- **You know someone influential on the board or involved with the internal workings of the school.**

What if you don't have a red carpet voucher?

If you're not breathing the same rarified air as the student's with red carpet vouchers, it's OK. You just have to apply like most people do. If you aren't getting a voucher, you need to survive stage two:

Stage Two: Shallow Metrics

Remember the dating analogy? It's back.

If the admissions officer doesn't know you from Adam, and no one is telling her that she needs to pay attention, then she will rely on *heuristics.* In this case: *your grades and test scores.*

If you have 10,000 potential spouses, all strangers, and a month to decide which one you get to marry, what's the first thing you'll do to make your life easier? Eliminate the ones that you don't find physically attractive enough. Shallow, but true.

What do colleges find sexy? Grades and test scores.

Having really bad grades or SAT/ACT scores is like showing up to a dating event wearing a wig made out of rotten spinach.

"But wait until you hear my ideas for the future of alternative energy!"

If you're wearing a spinach wig, you're not getting that far.

My whole life, I've tried to be a nice person. And I don't like to be the bearer of bad news. But if you don't have someone vouching for you, and your grades and scores aren't very good, then *you simply do not have a chance of getting into an extremely competitive school*. It won't happen. It *doesn't* happen.

What about score-optional colleges?

Score-optional colleges still require high GPAs. However, they don't "require" test scores. They'll look at your application without SAT/ACT scores submitted and still give it a fair shake.

Sounds amazing, right? You can just skip your SAT/ACT prep and apply to these schools, right!?

Not really. Because when schools become score-optional, two things happen:

1. **Score-optional schools get MORE APPLICANTS with BETTER QUALIFICATIONS.** You're not the only one who noticed that they're score optional. Every single kid with a great GPA, amazing extracurriculars, and so-so SAT/ACT scores is applying. That means that you're against a *larger, tougher field of applicants*. You don't have to submit your test scores, but so what? Your chances aren't any better. In fact, they're often worse. You're just competing against all the extra kids with amazing abilities who happen to have low test scores who are applying because of the school's score-optional status. And make no mistake: EVERY school that goes score-optional gets WAY more applicants.

2. **Score-optional colleges often have BETTER average SAT/ACT scores than their "score required" counterparts.** Remember: they're not "no-score" colleges, they're "score-optional." That means that if you have amazing scores, you can still submit them. And the kids with amazing scores *do* still submit them. And these colleges still *really care*, because higher scores still improve their rankings. They get the best of all worlds: kids submitting amazing scores when they have them, and incredible applicants on the other side of the equation *without* the low scores to drag down their averages.

As far as I'm concerned, the entire "score optional" thing is a total scam - it's a PR move designed to make schools look benevolent and fair-minded, when they're actually just improving their average scores and the size of their applicant pools. Anyone who tells you otherwise is probably working for one of these colleges.

If you're still interested in learning more about this whole scam, here's the list of "score optional" colleges, put together by Fair Test:

http://www.fairtest.org/university/optional

I don't see score-optional colleges as any sort of solution to low SAT and ACT scores. If you don't have high scores, *start getting them - NOW*.

The entire process is much simpler than most people believe, and if you put in just 15-30 minutes a day, you can get significantly higher scores in a surprisingly short period of time. But until you start studying, you'll never be able to improve. We'll tackle this subject in depth later on.

In summary, you need good metrics. When you go on a first date, you need to look your best. When you apply to a college without a red carpet voucher and you don't have good metrics, you're out of luck.

If you do not have high SAT/ACT scores, you need to either:

A) Raise your scores
B) Lower your standards
And/Or:
C) Apply to score-optional schools and pray for the best

If you do not have high grades, you need to:

A) Raise your grades
Or:
B) Lower your standards

That's all there is to it. If you have a 2.1 GPA and you're not red carpeted, you simply aren't going to a top twenty school. It isn't happening.

I don't say this to be cruel. I say this to save you time and emotional distress down the line. I don't want you getting your hopes up for no reason.

Also: if your grades and scores are WAY higher than the school's averages, you're VERY likely (though never guaranteed) to get in.

Because applications are so ludicrously competitive nowadays, having grades and scores way above the averages of your target schools is somewhat rare. But it does happen from time to time. For instance, when I was in high school, and the SAT was still scored out of 1600, a certain European college trying to recruit members of my graduation class pretty much flat-out said that if we broke a 1300, they'd let us in (barring a hate crime on our resumes).

If you have a 3.9 average and a 35 on your ACT, and you're applying to a college with an average entering GPA of 2.9 and ACT score of 22 - congratulations! You're probably accepted. Just apply to a few school like that, remembering that admissions is *always* a crapshoot, and then set your sights a bit higher.

For everyone else, keep reading.

If your grades and scores aren't high enough, you get chopped. However, once you make the cut (and we'll discuss that cut, where it is, and how to beat it in the next two chapters), you can move on to stage three:

YOU

Yes, you! The man in the mirror! The living, breathing human being whose personal qualities should have been considered in the first place.

If you don't have a red carpet voucher, but your grades and scores are good enough, *then* the admissions officers will take a look at what you have to offer. Your extracurriculars. Your essays. Your recommendations. All that good stuff!

What kind of "you" are they trying to uncover? The kind of "you" that will offer them something that they want.

We'll get through all of that in Section Four. For now, however, we need to take care of the most important things first. This book is called <u>Why You Get Rejected</u> for a reason: before we do the stuff that *gets you in*, we need to avoid the stuff that'll get you chopped. And for that, we move on to the next chapter...

CHAPTER 10

Your GPA: The Metric Man's Metric

Most of the time, I try to avoid making obvious statements. But this one is necessary:

To get into a good college, you need good grades.

Colleges care about grades more than anything else, and for very good reason. Good grades show colleges that you have ONE thing going for you:

When you have good grades, colleges see that **the combination of your intelligence and your work ethic allows you to successfully tackle diverse challenges.**

We all know that "dumb" guy in class who gets perfect grades because he works his butt off. We also know that "really smart" guy who gets horrible grades because he doesn't give a crap. Hence, grades don't reflect *intelligence* OR *work ethic* - they reflect <u>*the product of the two.*</u>

What do colleges want? People who can contribute a lot to their communities while they're present, and who can donate a lot of money when they're gone.

Who contributes a lot? People who are smart and work hard (in whatever combination delivers the best results). Whether you have a lazy, genius writer who's still able to pump out Pulitzer-quality work for the school paper, or a "dumb" scientist who spends 80 hours a week in the lab, you're going to end up with someone who *contributes*. Grades are the best indicator of this.

Who makes a lot of money? Usually, the people who combine their intelligence and work ethic to *get the job done*. Why do you think employers care so much about GPA? It's an *indicator*. Not everyone with a high GPA does well in life, and not everyone with a low GPA does poorly (entrepreneurs like myself are usually the exception in that case), but *a high GPA USUALLY leads to success in whatever field you choose*. It's a good bet.

Colleges don't like taking stupid risks. Admissions officers don't have time NOT to rely on heuristics. As a result, **your GPA is the most important part of your entire application.**

There is, of course, one exception: if you have a red carpet voucher. I'm a case in point. When I applied to college, I had garbage grades. I had a 4.0 average, which sounds impressive, except that at my high school, the grading scale was out of 6. I was in the bottom fourth of my class.

So how the heck did I get into an Ivy? I was one of the top rowing prospects in the country. The Columbia crew coach basically told the admissions officers to let me in no matter what, so they did. It didn't hurt that I had really good SAT scores, since I also lent a hand to their overall statistics - and it also didn't hurt that I had good recommendations and a strong extracurricular profile (I was the head editor of my school's comedy paper), but *without the crew voucher, there is a zero percent chance that I would have gotten into Columbia.*

Because of crew, I ended up getting into *two* different Ivies: Columbia and Cornell. But here's what's interesting: of the fourteen colleges I applied to that *weren't* Ivies, I got rejected from almost *all* of them.

How is that possible? How did I get into two of the best schools in the country, and rejected from so many others that were so much "worse?" *Because the other schools didn't have crew programs and I didn't get a voucher - therefore, the FIRST thing they noticed about me was my grades. And guess what happened?*

CHOP.

Example: I got rejected from Davidson College. As of the time of writing this, <u>Davidson was the #9 liberal arts college in the country, and it had a 21% admission rate.</u> It's a damn good school.

<u>But Columbia has a 7.0% admission rate, and it's the #4 overall university in the country.</u>

The reason that Davidson didn't let me is because *they didn't want my crew skills – I had nothing to offer them up front. As a result, they relied on heuristics, saw my grades, and I got cut before they ever learned anything else about me.*

I'm beating a dead horse, so I'll stop, but just remember: grades above all. If you don't have a voucher, then you need good grades or you'll get rejected.

You know you need good grades. Obviously. The real question is, how do you get them? The answer is actually a bit more strategic than you might think.

In poker, it doesn't matter how good you are if you play lots of crappy hands to start. Over the long run, you'll end up losing. And in academics, it doesn't matter how smart or diligent you are if you *take the wrong classes*. So, before we address any other tactics, let's *first* look at the starting point: *the classes that you take.*

Picking the Right Classes

Want to get good grades? Then don't take classes that set you up for failure.

You want to show colleges that you're smart and hard working - these are admirable qualities, and taking challenging classes *should* reflect this - but if you *bomb* them, then you're just shooting yourself in the foot!

Remember: *admissions officers don't have time to learn all about you. They need to take shortcuts. Therefore, **if your GPA stinks, they usually won't take the time to find out why!***

This is a conversation that *does not* take place:

"Sure, the kid has a 2.0 average - but I mean, he takes Chinese, Latin, quantum physics, and all AP classes - good for him! What a guy! Who cares if he has horrible grades? He's really shooting for the moon!"

Here's the conversation that actually takes place:

"Hmmmm.....2.0? [sound of folder being tossed in a trashcan]."

Before the massive uproar of angry college consultants begins, let me make something else clear:

ONCE YOU AVOID THE CHOPPING BLOCK, colleges do care a lot about the difficulty level of your classes. If you take nothing but "facts about bears" and arts and crafts class, you're not going to look particularly serious. But you need to *prioritize*. In other words: *only take really tough classes if you can actually manage them.* It's way better to survive the first round, *then* explain away some easier classes, than it is to pull your own application out of the trash can. **Once you're dead, you're dead.**

With that in mind, here's my advice for selecting the right classes:

1. **Start with the easiest ones you can, and focus on crushing them.**
2. **If you find that you can easily get an A in a certain class, consider taking the AP version.**
3. **Don't take Latin or Chinese.**

Skip to the next paragraph if you don't take either of these languages and you're not considering them. If you are, keep reading. I took Latin in high school. It destroyed me. I'm actually really good at languages, but Latin isn't a language - it's an exercise in GPA destruction. And in case anyone out there tries to tell you that it'll help with your SAT scores (because of vocabulary) - it won't. Just forget it. I speak from experience. Do not take Latin. Learn an actual language that you can actually use in your real life - what a treat! And as for Chinese - it's just way too hard for most native English speakers to tackle during high school. I'm all about challenging the brain - it's a fantastic and necessary exercise. But do it later in life, when you're not completely sabotaging your application prospects.

The idea is simple: start easy, then build up once you figure out what you're good at. Don't tackle complex challenges for no reason. If you realize that you have a knack for science, take AP physics. If you're crushing Spanish, take AP Spanish. But don't enroll in really hard classes until you know you're going to do well.

Taking tough classes and getting bad grades is like showing up at a dating event smelling like cheese, then trying to explain to women that the *reason* you smell like cheese is because *you're extremely fancy, and have a taste for fine cheeses.*

Seriously. It's that bad.

Take the toughest classes you possibly can, *so long as you can maintain a good GPA.*

What's good? Depends on the college, but the higher, the better. Look into your target schools' average incoming GPAs and plan accordingly. Ideally, you'll be in the upper range.

One other thing before we get into **how to get good grades:** you need to get them *at all times.*

Every Year Matters - Lay the Foundation Early, and Keep It Up!

Way too many of my students have the same story:

"Well, I sort of bombed freshman year, and I didn't take sophomore year very seriously, but this year, I've been doing great!"

The problem with this "strategy" is that *averages are very tough to budge.*

If you have a 3.0 your freshman and sophomore year, and a 4.0 your junior year, you're going to be applying with a 3.33. That's not very good.

Much easier to just maintain a 3.5 the whole time, no?

But isn't it true that colleges like to see an "upward trend?"

No! Colleges don't like to see an "upward trend" - **they like to see consistent excellence!**

This is one of the most infuriating myths out there, and one that I hear all the time. I can't tell you how many parents have said the same thing to me: "Well, Joey needed some adjusting in his freshman and sophomore years, so his grades aren't very good overall, but he's really excelling now, and I think that colleges will notice that things are on the up and up!"

This isn't "good" - it's *better than being consistently horrible.*

Of course, the *worst* thing that you can do is start with good grades, then start slipping. This is a very, very worrying trend. It shows colleges that you started out strong, couldn't handle the pressure of high school, and started cracking under that pressure. Think about what this hints at re: your performance in college, which will be consistently more demanding than high school.

This really boils down to one message: don't get complacent. Don't assume that you can bomb a class or two and "make them up later." Bad grades haunt you, and they *permanently* drag down your entire GPA. Give it your all, and keep at it no matter what. **There is nothing harder to overcome than bad grades.** Therefore, an ounce of prevention is worth a pound of remedy.

This all sounds fine, but there's an elephant in the room: *how do you get better grades?* How do you make sure that you're doing everything necessary to keep your GPA up in both your good and your bad subjects? Good question.

How to Get Good Grades

This subject is obviously beyond the scope of this book. The two *most* important things are to *take the right classes* and to *get your sleep (which I cover in depth in my book, Test Prep for Parents)*. However, I do have a few other tips that'll make a big difference.

There are countless books, courses, etc. out there that'll help you to improve your GPA (and I'll provide a list of my favorites at the end of this chapter). But if you want my "quick and dirty" secrets for an enhanced GPA, follow the advice below. It's all very simple, very effective, and makes an enormous difference in my students' GPAs.

Step One: Open up lines of communication with your teachers. Almost every time a student of mine has a really bad grade in a particular subject, it's the same story:

"The teacher is a jerk, he stinks at teaching, and he has it in for me."

I don't know the teacher, and I can't say whether this is true or whether it's in my student's head, but I do know this: *there is a serious communication issue here.*

If you have an adversarial (or nonexistent) relationship with your teacher, your grades will suffer. And the way to fix that is to approach your teacher politely and earnestly and figure out two things:

    A)   *What can I be doing better in this class? How can I meet your expectations more effectively?*
    B)   *Can you help me to understand the things that are giving me trouble?*

If you take the time to attend office hours, pre-class meetings, or just go out of your way to make a meeting with your teacher and get these questions answered, you'll be making enormous strides. At this point, many teachers and parents might roll their eyes: "Yeah, yeah, but won't the teachers see through this? Won't they just think of it as sucking up?"

If it is sucking up, and it's not earnest, then sure they will. But if you're actually trying to meet your teachers' expectations, and understand their material, they'll appreciate it. How will they know the difference?

    A)   If you ask a teacher what he wants from you, get a straight answer, and then do it, you'll earn his respect. Oftentimes, the students who think their teachers "have it in for them" find out that their teachers just can't read their handwriting, or don't like that they sit in the back of class and don't participate. They make small changes, and they revolutionize their GPA.

If your teacher tells you what he wants you to change, and you don't do it - that's your problem. You deserve a bad grade. If his demands are irrational, or if they're rational, you follow them, and then he still gets mad, you have grounds to switch classes. But *find out what your teacher wants and then make a serious effort to give it to him.*

B)   This is the ultimate area where teachers know if you're serious, or if you're just a suck-up. If you ask questions they've already answered in class, then it's obvious that you're just screwing around and not paying attention. This will tick them off. But if you go with a question like this:
"I know that you explained how photosynthesis works under these conditions - but I really don't get why it happens at different rates if X Y and Z factors are the same. I read the assigned text, did the homework, and listened to X explanation, but it's really troubling me. Would you mind walking me through it?"

That's a good question. You'll learn what you need to, and you'll make your teacher happy. Your teacher can also point you in the direction of other resources that'll make quite a big difference. It's just like a college interview - if you go in and ask questions that anyone can Google, you'll look like a joke. If you go in and ask questions that demonstrate your research and diligence, you'll build a strong relationship.

So, step one is to build lines of communication with your teacher, establish expectations, and ask well-researched questions.

Step Two: Improve your time management. There's no difference between time management at school and in the workplace. And when it comes to time management, only three things really matter: advanced planning, prioritization, and self-imposed time deadlines. Here's how they work in the academic setting:

1.   **See the big picture and figure out your goals and your workload for the long and short term.** If you view all of your schoolwork as one giant, shapeless blob, you'll end up with bad grades. You won't know what to prioritize, how far in advance to plan for essays, tests, etc., and you'll end up stressed out of your mind.

You should take a month-long look at ALL your classes, every month, and figure out what's expected of you. When are the tests? Quizzes? When are the papers due? When are group projects due? How much homework do you have for each class a night, on average? Factor it all in and figure out precisely when it's going to get done.

Don't be an ostrich and stick your head in the sand. Sure, it's a bit daunting to look at all your work at once, but it's way better than getting blindsided by it every single day, with no preparation for especially heavy days (and no way to maximize particularly light days).

Use your syllabi and figure this all out. You should have a map for the whole term. And by the way, if your teachers don't provide good syllabi, it's a great way to open up another line of communication and ask them when the big stuff is due. No teacher is going to get angry because you're planning ahead.

Once you do this, you'll be able to move to step two:

2. **Prioritize on a daily basis, and use a calendar rather than a to-do list.**
    To-do lists *can be* fantastic, but they're often unrealistic and ineffective. How often have you crafted an ambitious, amazing to-do list, only to go to sleep with 9/10ths of the items undone (or even more items on it than there were when you started)?

This isn't an uncommon experience - practically everyone who uses to-do lists falls into the same trap. Though I'm an obsessive to-do list keeper, I stopped using them years ago. I found something far more effective.

My productivity routine now contains only two elements:

First, I figure out *three*, and only *three*, things that I *really* need to get done in a given day. Anything else is just icing on the cake. So long as I can complete my three big tasks, I'm good to go.

Second, I *use a calendar to schedule those tasks into exact time slots that I force myself to commit to.*

Here's how this works:

First, I decide that in a given day, before I do anything else, I'm going to opti-
mize the geometry curriculum in my software, write a rough draft chapter of
my new book, and re-design my video series for my YouTube channel. Those
are the big priorities. Everything else is cool, but not necessary.

Second, I actually slot those activities into my calendar, like so:

9-9:45am - Work on geometry optimization
Break
10-10:45am - Work on the book
Break
11-11:45am - Design video series
Gym and lunch
1-1:30pm - continue optimizing geometry
Break
1:45-2:30pm - Work on book
Break
2:45-3:30pm - Work on book
Break
4pm-6pm - finish optimization of software and outsource to developer
6:30pm - dinner with friends

There's nothing particularly fancy about this. And that's the whole point. It's *simple*,
and the simplicity is what makes it work. I don't have some vague idea of when I'll be
doing what. Furthermore, I know exactly how much time I'm giving to each task. I can
be realistic. If I only had one slot to write a chapter of the book, I'd know I was lying to
myself and I'd reorder things to make them more realistic.

*Most importantly, putting your key priorities on your calendar forces you to COMMIT
to your designated work times like actual appointments.* Nature loves a vacuum,
and if you don't schedule your most essential tasks, you'll end up getting your
most important time filled with random, unimportant junk (emails, Facebook,
little "check off this task but it doesn't actually get you anywhere" jobs, unplanned
phone calls, etc.). If you commit to this sort of scheduling, and force yourself to

stick with it, you won't need to worry about random outside demands and distractions taking up your time.

The difference between effective and ineffective people: effective people are *proactive*, and ineffective people are *reactive*. Effective students set their priorities, set their schedules, and get things done. Ineffective students react to any random stimuli that cross their path, and as a result, they never put their effort where it needs to be. *They never use the time they have because it's always getting stolen from them. <u>And they're letting it happen.</u>*

If you use this same technique for your academics, you'll experience a renaissance. You'll realize that you have a *lot* more time than you realized. You'll also realize that when you prioritize and plan ahead, you'll never be sideswiped by "unexpected" tests and papers, never stay up late on last-minute projects, and never feel stressed.

The Other Goodies

The above tips (pick the right classes, get some sleep, prioritize, set your calendar for the day, and think ahead) are the most important. For more tactical goodness, I have six books that I'm sort of obsessed with. I have no connection with their authors, and I make no money if you buy them - they're just awesome, and I either use them myself on a daily basis, or recommend them to all my own students who have GPA troubles:

1. <u>**Getting Things Done, by David Allen.**</u> The greatest productivity book ever. Read it, live it, love it.
2. <u>**How to Become a Straight-A Student by Cal Newport.**</u> Good lord do I love this book. Buy it, read it, use it. Cal is a bit of a legend when it comes to improving GPAs, and for good reason.
3. <u>**The One Thing by Gary Keller.**</u> Life-changing. Kids and adults *need* to read this.
4. <u>**Triple Your Reading Speed by Wade E. Cutler.**</u> No ability is more useful, or less understood, than speed-reading. In my opinion, speed-reading is a *requirement* in today's society, and students who don't know how to do it are at a massive disadvantage. If you don't know how to do it, take the time. It's foolish not to.

5. **The 80/20 Principle by Richard Koch.** This is one of my favorite books of all time. It will change the way you view the world (and has a lot to do with The One Thing, as you'll see when you read it).

6. **The Four Hour Chef by Tim Ferriss.** Ostensibly, this book is about cooking. Really, it's about how to learn *anything*, and how to do it as efficiently as effectively as possible. I'm a huge Tim Ferriss fan, and this book is, by far, his best. I suppose I should warn potential readers that it includes references to sex, anatomy, some pretty gruesome hunting photos, and profanity galore - but if you're OK with those things, then man oh man, do you need to read this book.

You'll notice that only one of the books above has anything to do with actual academics. That's because *the key to getting good grades is* _learning how to learn_. These books are fun to read, teach you awesome life-applicable skills, and, above all else, show you that *learning, in and of itself, is an awesome habit that can always be improved.*

Your GPA Is the Most Important Part of Your Application

Act accordingly! Fortunately, if you already have your list of dream schools, you'll have all the motivation you need to get in gear, and if you use all the advice above and combine it with the teachers at your school, you'll have all the tools you need to perform at your highest level. Now that that's out of the way, let's focus on my favorite subject in the universe: test prep!

CHAPTER 11

You're Not Just a Number! Actually...You Kind of Are

> *"...democracy is the worst form of Government - except for all those other forms that have been tried from time to time...."*
> — *WINSTON CHURCHILL*

This chapter is about standardized tests. Get ready for some fun!

I started the chapter with that Churchill quote for a reason - standardized tests are the worst, most useless, dehumanizing, demoralizing, wretched ways possible to figure out the worthiness of applicants - except for every other way that colleges have tried so far.

Countless studies have shown that SAT and ACT scores have almost nothing to do with college readiness or future success. A lot of people are really surprised to hear that I agree with this statement wholeheartedly.

The *idea* behind standardized tests is pretty simple: since all schools are different, only *standardized tests* provide a *standard, objective* way of figuring out how smart and capable kids are. After all, a 4.2 at one school might be a 3.2 at another - but a 2210 on the SAT is a 2210 on the SAT no matter where the heck you happen to come from. Makes sense, right?

Sort of.

From what I've seen, there are two far more obvious reasons why schools use standardized tests in the admissions process:

1. **They save admissions officers time.**
    Remember: there's no such thing as "Cornell" or "Vanderbilt" - just a bunch of humans who work to keep those concepts going. The admissions process is a human process. And if humans find a way to save time and effort, they'll use it. Why the heck would these officers spend countless hours *truly* evaluating the merit of every student when they can use numbers instead?

    And before you think I'm knocking admissions officers, I'm not - I know sweet, caring admissions officers who work their tails off - I'm just pointing out an obvious fact about human nature and the realities of the administrative process. SAT and ACT scores are a heuristic mechanism. And *everyone* needs heuristic mechanisms if they want to avoid going insane.

2. **They tell colleges which applicants have money.**
    I've been *severely* criticized for saying this before, and I'm sure I'll be severely criticized again. But people usually yell the loudest when the barbs pierce closest to the heart. Here's the ugly truth:

    <u>SAT and ACT scores are a LINEAR indicator of how wealthy a student is.</u>

    I'm not saying that they're *correlated* - I'm saying that *rich kids <u>almost always</u> get higher SAT and ACT scores than do poor kids.* It's screwed up. But it's the way it is.

    Remember that really important thing that I told you was most loved by colleges? Money? Well...there happens to be a pretty good way of figuring out whether or not someone has it: look at his SAT or ACT scores.

    There is no such thing as a "need-blind" college; colleges can figure out how much money you have by looking at your test scores!!!

Almost all colleges review applications and make admissions decisions *before* they look at parental income and scholarship considerations. How sweet. The thing is, it would be a lot sweeter if *they weren't just using different ways of figuring out how rich you are.*

Colleges want students who can pay full tuition. When they get those students, they make more money. But it would look pretty gross if they hung up a banner saying that they didn't want poor people to apply. How insensitive!

So instead, they just look for *every imaginable indicator* that will let them know that you're wealthy and can afford tuition.

"Oh - we don't need you to be rich - we're just looking for students who attend elite prep schools with perfect SAT scores, 4.2 weighted GPAs, and whose parents have the time and resources to take them to hockey practice!"

Give me a break.

Does *every* kid with high SAT scores end up being rich? No. Does *every* kid with low SAT scores end up being underprivileged? No. But *the vast majority of the time, they do.* And when you're admitting thousands of kids at a time, the statistics level out in your favor.

Here's what's really screwed up: SAT and ACT scores have almost nothing to do with intelligence or ability. There's a reason why all of my students get such enormously improved test scores: *every* student is capable of getting high SAT and ACT scores *with the right coaching and curriculum.* When my students tell me they're "bad at math," or "bad at reading," I love proving them wrong. What they really mean is that "they're not *yet* comfortable with the math or reading challenges that these tests force them to overcome." Learn the facts and figures, learn the tricks and strategies, and bam - you have high scores.

But guess what? Coaching and curriculum usually cost a lot of time and money. And the effects of coaching and curriculum are built upon an academic base that *also* costs a lot of time and money to build. For instance, my one-on-one students all came from extremely wealthy families. Even when their test scores were initially very low, it was easy to raise them because they've been exposed to incredibly amazing educational resources their entire lives. They go to great schools, they have attentive parents and tutors, and they have (and have always had) all the resources that they need to thrive. They're very easy to help because they have incredibly strong educational foundations built beneath them.

Now take a student whose parents don't make a lot of money. As a result, he lives in lower-income area, and because his parents pay lower taxes, the public education available to him isn't geared toward the SAT. His parents can't afford extra tutoring, educational resources, etc. (and in many cases aren't aware of the more affordable options available), and so he goes for years without building up the necessary foundation to be able to utilize test prep lessons effectively. This causes a chain-reaction that leads to one inevitable conclusion: lower SAT scores.

These lower SAT scores say nothing about him, his intelligence, his work ethic, or his merit as a student or as a future contributor to society at large. But they sure do say a lot about his income. That's exactly why I sell my test prep software for a few hundred dollars (compared to the $1,500+ classes offered by most large firms and the $5,000 tutoring packages that they upsell more frequently) - it's a way of leveling the playing field.

Do colleges *only* care about test scores because they're income indicators? Of course not. They also show that you have certain math, reading, grammar, and logical reasoning skills that'll help you to get by in their classes. This way, they don't need to inflate grades (as much), and they can continue to pretend that they're largely responsible for your proficiency in life once you graduate.

So pick your poison. Colleges care so much about SAT and ACT scores because:

A) They show how amazing you are as a student and a human being
B) They show that you'll be able to hack it at their school
C) They show that you're "smart"

D) They show that you're probably rich
E) Some combination of the above

Whatever you believe about the reasons why colleges care so much, they do. A lot. Even at the score optional colleges, they're a big deal.

Fortunately, regardless of how screwed up this entire scenario might be, *you have a way around it.* You can beat the tests that these schools require. All it takes is a little bit of planning and preparation combined with *consistent effort.* But anyone can do it, and it doesn't need to cost an arm and a leg (or anywhere near it).

In the chapters that follow, I'll show you exactly *which test to take, when to take it,* and *how to prepare.*

Colleges use test scores to chop people - plain and simple. By the end of this section, you'll know how to avoid the axe. Let's get to it, shall we?

CHAPTER 12

The Big Guns - The PSAT, SAT, and ACT

To get into a competitive school, you need high SAT or ACT scores. Before you begin prepping, I want you to understand what these tests are, how they're different, and how to set your testing schedule properly. When it comes to SAT and ACT prep, planning is *everything*.

First, we need to bring up the PSAT. Before you take the official SAT or the ACT, you'll often end up taking the "dry run" version of the SAT first. This isn't ideal: *you should start and finish your test prep as early as possible. This is the most essential ingredient in high test scores.* But, unfortunately, many students are *first* exposed to the SAT via the PSAT during their sophomore and junior year.

The PSAT is offered by your high school during the fall of your sophomore year. The College Board usually publishes upcoming PSAT dates here (you can also get a fee waiver for the $14 fee if need be):

http://professionals.collegeboard.com/testing/psat/about/dates

The PSAT is also offered in the fall of your junior year. This is the one that *really* matters, as we'll discuss shortly. Before I tell you how to deal with it, you should first understand the *purpose* of this test.

What is the PSAT, and what's the point of taking it sophomore year?

The point of taking this test your sophomore year is pretty basic: to let you know where you stand. The PSAT is almost *exactly* the same thing as the SAT. The questions, formatting, material, etc., on each "practice" test are practically identical to their "real deal" counterparts.

The only three differences between the PSAT and the SAT are:

1. The PSAT is shorter - about half as long as the real thing.
2. The PSAT doesn't have an essay.
3. The PSAT is graded on a slightly different scale.

Key note: do NOT purchase practice materials, programs, or anything else made specifically for the PSAT - just get the materials for the actual SAT instead.

There's no difference between the tests except that the practice versions are shorter. Anyone selling PSAT-specific materials is just banking on the fact that you don't know the difference, like Excedrin selling "Excedrin Migraine" even though it's exactly the same thing as regular Excedrin.

The grading element is the only thing that requires a bit of explanation. The New SAT is scored from 400-1600 points, with 200-800 points awarded for the math section and another 200-800 points awarded for the reading+writing section. The PSAT will be scored from 320-1520 points, with 160-760 points awarded for the math section and 160-760 points awarded for the reading+writing section. Why the difference? According to the College Board, it's to show that the PSAT is easier than the SAT, and hence you can't get the same high scores. This is stupid - just take whatever PSAT scores you get, multiply them by 1.05, and you'll get your predictive SAT score.

So *what's the point of taking them sophomore year?* As I said: just to give you an idea of where you stand. I actually got a *horrible* PSAT score, which alerted my mother to my horrible innate testing abilities. She made me prep like a lunatic, and I ended up with a 99th percentile SAT score. The PSAT did its job.

Your sophomore-year scores on the PSAT are JUST FOR YOU. They don't get submitted to colleges, no one sees them, and they don't actually *matter*. This is a *practice exam* in the purest sense of the word "practice."

So why take it in the first place?

1. **Experience.** Nothing beats the experience of actually sitting in a testing center, building up your nerves, and seeing how you do. Much like riding a rollercoaster, taking an official test is only scary the first time. After that, you're used to it. This way, you don't have to go into the real testing environment "cold" and full of nerves.

2. **Familiarity.** For a lot of kids, the PSAT will be their *only* exposure to the material and formatting of this test before they take the real thing. Sad but true, considering how easy this tests is to beat. By giving the practice versions of these tests once, the College Board can at least say that the kids who take the real exams all *know the rules*. It would be pretty unfortunate if you had to figure out the *rules* of each section *on your first try, while the clock was running*. So that's nice, I guess.

Fortunately for you, the PSAT isn't particularly necessary. You'll be getting *plenty* of practice, familiarity, experience, and training on your own - IF you start prepping early, as we'll discuss shortly.

All you really need to know about the **sophomore year PSAT** is this: it's a nice bit of practice to show you where you stand, but it doesn't really matter.

However, the **junior year PSAT is a different story.**

National Merit Scholarships and the Junior Year PSAT

Students are allowed to take the PSAT once a year. But only in their junior year does the PSAT really matter. That's because **the junior year PSAT is submitted to the National Merit Scholarship Corporation**, and **students who get really good PSAT scores can become National Merit Finalists.**

To learn all about this organization, check out their website here:

http://www.nationalmerit.org/entering.php

I won't go into too much depth, so if you have any unanswered questions, check that link. Here's everything you really need to know about the PSAT and the National Merit scenario:

1. **To become a finalist, you need to get 98th percentile PSAT scores or better.** Yes, that's right - if you want to be a finalist, you need to beat 49/50 people in your state. This isn't easy.
   If your initial scores (discussed shortly) aren't in this ballpark, then don't sweat it – it's really not worth going for the National Merit Finalist status unless you're close to being there already. If you're close, then it's worth shooting for.

   What's a 98th percentile PSAT score? It depends on the state. Just Google "[your state] National Merit scores" and find out. It's high.

2. **If you become a National Merit Finalist, you can win money.** Which is pretty cool.
   http://www.collegedata.com/cs/content/content_payarticle_tmpl. jhtml?articleId=10126

   College Data has a pretty thorough breakdown if you want to check it out. You can win anywhere from $2,500 to practically your entire tuition.

   The first scholarship - the one from the National Merit board itself - is automatic. The other scholarships usually have to do with your financial scenario.

3. **If you don't get a National Merit Finalist spot, it's not a big deal.**
   Remember: only 1/50 people get to this level, and not all of them end up qualifying all the way through. This is still the PRACTICE SAT after all, and it's not really something you need to sweat about. Real SAT and ACT scores matter way more.

4. **If you DO get one of these scholarships, it looks DARN good on your application.** School rankings are partly decided by the number of National Merit Finalists who attend, and so schools are always eager to snatch them up - it's a

badge of honor. They sure do love that reputation boost. While a National Merit Finalist isn't a shoe-in anywhere, he'll have a little extra juice on his application, and, most likely, his application will get tagged with a little "NMSQT" badge that shows who he is, which will usually get him past round one with more ease - colleges will overlook certain flaws in an application to scoop a Merit Finalist.

Here's the funny thing, though: **if you get a National Merit Finalist-level PSAT score, it means you're going to get an awesome SAT score, so it's sort of a moot point!**

Think about it: all the PSAT is supposed to do is show what you *will* score on the SAT! So if you get a fantastic PSAT score, it's pretty much just an indication that you'll get a fantastic SAT score. And the real deal matters more anyway.

So what the heck should do you do!?

OK, so now we know what the PSAT is, when it's given, and what it accomplishes. But the big question still remains: what the heck do you do about it?

Nothing. Nothing at all.

You shouldn't be preparing for the PSAT - you should simply be preparing for the SAT!

If you're prepared for the real test(s), you'll be prepared for the practice tests, so there's really no purpose in worrying about them at all. And **the sooner you start preparing for the real tests and get them out of the way, the better off you'll be.**

The SAT is just a longer version of the PSAT - so why not train for the harder one? You'll just do better on the shorter one. It makes no sense to focus on the practice versions of this test.

Instead, your focus should be on the real deal. Which brings up the next big question:

When do you start prepping for the ACT/SAT?

My answer always has been, and always will be, *as soon as possible*. But let me get a bit more specific:

Freshman year. You should start your *freshman year*. If it's your freshman year, start now. If it's later than your freshman year, start now.

But won't you learn tons of stuff in school that'll help you on the SAT and ACT? Won't it be better to wait!? Not really. In fact, **most of my students have to UNLEARN a lot of what they've been taught in high school in order to do well on the SAT and ACT.** Most American high schools (even extremely good ones) don't do very much to help students prepare for these exams. Grammar is barely taught at all, reading comprehension skills aren't honed much from year to year, and even math isn't really taught in a way that enhances SAT and ACT scores.

Math, in particular, is *damaged* by extra time in high school. While students *do* cover certain geometry, algebra, and precalculus concepts in high school, they also *forget* a lot of the more basic stuff that comes up *constantly* on the SAT and ACT - stuff like fractions, exponents, remainders, etc. Each year of schooling gives my students a few new skills, but it also allows them to forget a few others. On balance, I'd say it's about a wash.

With all that said, **the absolute best time to prepare for the SAT and ACT is your freshman year of high school.** You have all the time in the world to prepare,, you don't have to worry about any impending testing deadlines, and you don't have any other application considerations to deal with.

"But won't this be too stressful? Isn't starting this early a "tiger mom" move!?

Here's the thing: most people think of test prep as some ballistic, all-or-nothing "crash course," because that's what most prep firms sell. They imagine dragging themselves to classroom courses for four hours every weekend, studying for hours a day, and ruining their lives. But this is the *worst possible way to prep.*

The best way to study for the SAT and ACT is *slow and steady.* Put in 15-30 minutes a day, every day, broken up into small chunks. If you can put in just *15 minutes* *of prep a day* starting your freshman year, you'll have over *100 hours of prep experience by the end of your sophomore fall* - that's more than enough time to raise your scores by entire college tiers!

There isn't a student alive who can't find *15 minutes a day to prep.* And because your brain learns best through consistent, long-term study, you're not just getting this process out of the way early - you're actually studying *more effectively* than the unfortunate students who sign up for those ridiculous test prep "crash courses."

Starting early *reduces stress.*

If you don't get the scores you're looking for by the beginning of your sophomore year, you can always spend more time prepping. You'll have more time to lay a material foundation, enhance your reading skills and speed, and gain familiarity with the tests. And unlike sports, in which adrenaline can help you, academics and intellectual tasks are always performed best when they're done in a relaxed setting. If it's your last chance to take the SAT/ACT before the application deadline, it's going to be insanely intense. If you know you have two more years...not so much.

If you are already in your freshman year, then it's time to get started NOW. As in, IMMEDIATELY. If you're beyond your freshman year, it's time to get started NOW. As in, immediately. Do NOT put this process off. The sooner you rip off the Band-Aid, the better.

Now that we know *when* to start prepping, we need to address the next big question:

Which Test Should You Prep For?

The most important part of the college application process is picking the right schools. *The* most important part of maintaining a high GPA is picking the right classes. It should come as no surprise, then, that *the* most important part of your test prep plan is *picking the right test!*

Neither the SAT nor the ACT is "easier" or "harder" than the other – but different types of students usually do MUCH better on one than they do on the other. So making the right decision here is absolutely essential.

I tutor both the SAT and the ACT, but my reputation has been built in the SAT space. Therefore, parents usually come to me for SAT help – the ACT is something that they don't even consider. The opposite is also true: people coming to me for ACT prep rarely think of the SAT as an option.

This is problematic, because certain students are practically built to take the ACT, and will absolutely bomb the SAT – and vice versa.

Therefore, one of the first things I do when advising my clients is figure out which test I should be preparing their children for in the first place. Teaching an "ACT-style" student the SAT is like teaching someone with a sumo wrestler build how to perform ballet – there are limits to what you can accomplish.

Fortunately, the New SAT, launched in March of 2016, is practically identical to the ACT. While the Old SAT was very different from the ACT, the New SAT is extremely similar. This makes the decision much easier. However, picking the right test is still very important - you want to give yourself as much of an edge as possible!

First, let me discuss the differences between these two exams. Then, I'll show you how to figure out which one is right for you.

The Material Differences Between the SAT and the ACT

The SAT and the ACT test almost identical <u>material</u> – with a few key exceptions.

Both tests have essays. Both tests have math sections. Both tests have reading comprehension sections. Both tests have "grammar" sections. And, for the most part, the material tested by these sections is practically identical.

Learning the material for one exam will help you perform on the other. But there are a few exceptions:

A) **The New SAT emphasizes vocabulary SLIGHTLY more than the ACT does.** The Old SAT was *all about vocabulary*. The New SAT has removed almost all of its "vocabulary-specific" problems. That being said, it still has a few vocab tricks up its sleeve. A bigger vocabulary will be a slight advantage on the New SAT.

B) **The ACT tests slightly more complex, more advanced math.**
Both exams test almost identical mathematical material. You need a strong grasp on arithmetic, algebra, and geometry to thrive. But the ACT tosses in a few extras.

Roughly 9 out of the 60 problems on the ACT math section have to do with mathematical concepts that are barely covered on the New SAT, including trigonometry, imaginary numbers, advanced geometric shapes, logarithms, and more.

If you haven't covered these topics in school, the ACT will present additional challenges in the math section. None of these concepts are particularly hard to learn, but they present material that schools generally take up to a year to teach to their students (largely because classroom learning is so ludicrously ineffective).

If you're lagging in math at school, the ACT will probably be a bit harder on a material basis. If you're good at math, and you have a strong grasp on the more advanced topics, the ACT's material will be much easier.

The New SAT touches these subjects as well, but *barely*. All you really need to know to get a perfect New SAT score is *know what SohCahToa is* - on the ACT, you'll need to know how to use it in a variety of ways. But again - these differences are pretty minor.

C) **The SAT and ACT require identical grammatical and writing skills for the English / Writing sections, and for the essays.**
The *formatting* of both tests is *slightly* different, especially so for the essays, but there are no facts, figures, or formulas that you need to know for one test that you don't need to know for the other or vice versa.

D) **The ACT has a "science" section that has nothing – I repeat, NOTHING – to do with science.**
The ACT science section horrifies a lot of people. They think that it presents an entirely new sphere of knowledge that you need to master. This is not the case.

The ACT "science" section could more accurately be named the "using information in graphs and charts properly" section. It requires zero knowledge of chemistry, biology, physics, geology, etc. The ACT science section does require *strategy*, but the material on this section has nothing to do with science.

Example: an ACT science question might ask: "If birds had mass extinction events in 1234, 1754, and 1910, what might graph 3 suggest about the main cause of extinction for birds?"

Looking at graph 3, you'll see that there were massive increases in methane during the years 1230, 1750, and 1906. One of the answer choices will be: "Birds die from high methane concentrations in the air."

The next question will ask: "how long does it take for methane to kill birds?" One of the answers choices will be "4 years." If you notice that there is a 4-year gap between each methane leak and bird extinction, you're good to go. You don't have to know anything about methane and birds going into the test.

This isn't scientific knowledge – this is just common sense. But this section does take some getting used to. You need to figure out how to quickly and accurately decipher the graphs and charts presented. However, I can't emphasize this enough – you don't need to know any actual science to get a perfect ACT science score.

If the material is so similar, than what IS the difference between these tests?

Just because they test similar concepts does *not* mean that they're similar exams. The difference between these two tests comes down to one key concept:

The ACT is vastly more TIME-INTENSIVE.
The ACT is ludicrously time-rigorous.

Time management is *important* on the SAT – it is EVERYTHING on the ACT. Which, incidentally, is one of the main reasons why it's so much harder to get extra time on the ACT than it is on the SAT (a subject we'll cover in a later chapter).

I spend about 10% of my time with SAT students on time-management techniques. I spend about 70% of my time with ACT students on time-management techniques. The ACT is a test of timing. You need to fly through. You have far less time per question in each section, and you need to simply "pound it out."

Almost half a student's success on the ACT math section boils down to understanding which questions to skip. You have 60 minutes for 60 questions, all at once, and if you accidentally spend 6 minutes on question #17...kiss your score goodbye. That's at least 5 questions you won't get to answer.

The ACT gives you far less time per problem. Therefore, it is objectively "harder." So does this mean that you should just take the New SAT instead?

Not necessarily. Here's the thing: the New SAT gives *you* more time per problem. But it also gives *everyone else* more time per problem! Any comparative advantage between the two tests is destroyed by the fact that these tests are *graded on a scale*. The New SAT might be a bit easier than the ACT, but you're not graded on your *absolute performance* - you're graded on your performance *compared to the other students who take it.*

Therefore, if you can manage the time challenges delivered by the ACT, you have a big application edge!

If you don't need extra time, you're focused, and you have "sitting power" – the ability to plow through material without distraction – you have a HUGE advantage on the ACT. If you're easily distracted, have problems managing time, or get overwhelmed by pressure, you should avoid the ACT *at all costs*.

Again, you know yourself much better than I do. Can you sit down with 4 hours' worth of homework, emerge 4 hours later, and be finished? That's a somewhat rare ability, but if you have it – you will crush the ACT. If you have ADHD, or need a lot of breaks, or have trouble managing your time – the ACT will crush you. Stick with the SAT.

However, "anecdotal" suggestions aren't very helpful. Case in point: most of my students come to me thinking that they're "strong in math, and horrible at reading" – then, when they get their diagnostic tests back, their reading scores are better than their math scores, or all their scores are the same, or some other strange result comes up which defies all their own beliefs about their strengths and weaknesses.

When it comes to deciding between the SAT and the ACT, I prefer the facts.

However, before I tell you how to decide which test to take, I first want to make one very important point:

Colleges do NOT prefer one test to the other.

For some reason, there's a widespread belief that the ACT is some sort of "bohemian" exam. The "smart" kids take the SAT, and the "alternative" kids take the ACT. This concept is completely ridiculous.

Recently, the ACT surpassed the SAT as the most frequently taken college entrance exam. There is nothing alternative about the ACT whatsoever – especially now. And colleges couldn't care less which one you take – they just want high scores.

I think this belief stems from the fact that most parents never even heard of the ACT when they were applying to college. It was "SAT or bust." So this newer, more unfamiliar test strikes them as goofy and strange. But make no mistake: the ACT is plenty rigorous, and colleges know this.

I'm always asked which test certain colleges prefer, and my answer is always the same:

Colleges prefer high scores – that is all. Colleges simply use this chart to figure out how SAT and ACT scores compare:

http://www.act.org/solutions/college-career-readiness/compare-act-sat/

A 36 on the ACT is identical to a 1600 on the SAT. A 21 on the ACT is identical to a 1000 on the SAT. And so on and so forth.

When admissions officers look at an application, the process is the same: they check the student's GPA and his test scores, and if they're both high enough, they open the folder and read the rest. Whether those test scores are SAT or ACT scores is irrelevant – they just need to be high enough.

Key Note: There is ZERO point in taking *both* tests. Just figure out which test you're best at and take that one. Submitting a great SAT score and an equivalently great ACT score is like telling someone that you're 6 feet tall, but that you're also 2 yards tall. You're expressing the exact same point with different scales.

Horrible SAT/ACT scores will get you rejected. Extremely high SAT/ACT scores will get you through round one, win you scholarships, and make your life easier. And while it used to be the case that students who took the ACT didn't have to take SAT Subject Tests, this is no longer true, which lends zero advantage to either test.

Just take the test that you're better at taking, and all will be well.

With that in mind, we get to the punch line: how do you figure out which test you should take?

Which test you should take: Step One:

Get the official testing booklets for both exams. These books have real SATs and ACTs, and real grading rubrics. These are the two books:

Official College Board SAT Study Guide

You can also find all four of the tests in this book for free online here:

https://collegereadiness.collegeboard.org/sat/practice/full-length-practice-tests

The Real ACT Prep Guide

Step 2
Go through a full exam in each book on your own time. Before taking either practice test, you should get familiar with the basic formatting and question-types on each

exam. The point is to understand how much time you have on each section, figure out what's being asked, how the questions are formed, etc.

This could take up to five hours for each test. This isn't a quick or easy process – it's just the best process.

You shouldn't be going into these exams cold. You need to know what to expect, so that, during your practice tests, time isn't wasted just figuring out what the heck is going on.

Step 3
Set aside 4.5-hour blocks on two consecutive weekends and take a full, timed, graded diagnostic exam in each book.

To get an accurate idea of where you're scoring, you can't take these practice tests in split-up blocks, and you can't take them while distracted, at a school study hall, etc.

Create a quiet, well-lit test-taking environment at home, remove all distractions such as cell phones and TV, keep everyone out of the room, and make sure you're rested and well fed. Try to take both tests at the same time on the same day (i.e., 11am on a Sunday).

Step 4
Grade both exams. The books themselves have comprehensive, step-by-step grading manuals after each test. Once both tests are finished, you'll have a precise idea of where you're at on both tests.

Step 5
Compare the grades using this chart:

http://www.act.org/solutions/college-career-readiness/compare-act-sat/

For the time being, don't worry about the science section (it doesn't have a counterpart on the SAT, and it's very easily teachable). Just compare your reading, math, and writing/English scores, and use the chart above to do so.

If one score is significantly higher than the other, that's the test you're going to take.

If you get a 700 on your SAT math section, and a 22 on your ACT Math sections, you'll be taking the SAT. Done and done.

By "significant," I mean "more than about 100 total points difference on one test than the other."

Metrics are everything, and if you're clearly better at one test than the other based on real diagnostic exams, then you have your solution.

If you *hated* the ACT science section, and it made no sense to you, *take the SAT*. No point in learning an entirely new set of strategies and tactics if you don't have to. However, if you sort of liked it, and found that you had a natural knack for it, it could represent a giant edge. In that case, you'll probably want to lean toward the ACT.

If both scores are similar, pick the test you LIKED MORE.

I can promise you this: there WILL be a preference. After working with over 400 students one-on-one, and thousands more through my online software, I've never heard of a student who is "meh" on this topic. Students usually hate one test, and don't mind the other.

That's all there is to it.

Let metrics lead the way. If your ACT scores crush your SAT scores, then start prepping for the ACT immediately (and vice versa). If they're similar, pick the one you preferred taking. After seeing the "evils" of one test, you won't mind studying for the other nearly as much, and it'll help to enhance your motivation. You will perform better on one test than the other, and this is the best way to figure out which test is best.

Side note: if you already have PSAT scores, you can use those to compare to your ACT practice test score and save yourself the time of taking another practice SAT.

Whichever test put you in the highest percentile is the test you should study for, unless you had a violent aversion to one exam or the other.

WHEN should you take these tests?

This is another key point that you need to consider. Fortunately, the answer is actually much simpler than you might imagine.

You should take your SAT or ACT when the scores that you're getting on your practice exams are similar to the scores that you need to get into the colleges of your choice.

The *absolute worst* thing that you can do is "take a real test for the heck of it." DO NOT DO THIS. It's a very common practice, but it makes absolutely no sense. It's easy to figure out where you're scoring, and you shouldn't be walking into the testing center until you know precisely where you stand.

How do you take a proper practice exam? Two things are most important:

1. **Use actual test material.**
    Take real SATs from the The College Board Official SAT Study Guide and real ACTs from The Real ACT Prep Guide- not from third-party books and testing centers. If you want to know what a real test is like, and you want to get a real grade, take a real test with a real grading rubric.

    Save the material in your College Board and Real ACT books for diagnostic tests only.

2. **Take the tests under realistic conditions.**
    Get a proper night's sleep. Have a proper breakfast. Set aside all the time necessary. Turn off your phone, the radio, the computer, and the TV. Tell everyone in your house to leave you alone. Follow the timing guidelines and don't "cheat." Treat it as much like a real test as possible.

    A shameless plug: my online program teaches you exactly how to set up a proper self-testing environment, how to take these tests, prepare for them, grade them, analyze them, and use your results for future progress. If you want a full walkthrough, you can sign up for either program at https://green-testprep.com. **Also, you can use the code "WYGRcode" to get $25 off at checkout as a little "thank you" for buying this book!**

Don't take real tests unless you know that you're capable of getting the scores that you want. A lot of people worry about taking these tests multiple times. In reality, doing this isn't a very big deal. But you don't want to take them more times than you need to.

To figure out possible test dates, use these pages:

SAT Test Dates and Registration: http://sat.collegeboard.org/register/ sat-us-dates

ACT Test Dates and Registration: http://www.actstudent.org/regist/ dates.html

Both the SAT and ACT are offered at roughly the same times every single year, at multiple times throughout the year, with a long break between mid-June and early September. There are plenty of opportunities to take these tests.

No matter when you take the SAT or the ACT, just be sure of one thing: **register for a backup exam!** You ALWAYS want to do this. The reasons are incredibly numerous: the backup exam takes the pressure off, allows you to use super-scoring and score variance to get the best scores possible, and gives you an insurance policy in case you have an "off day" when taking the first test. Do not take only one SAT or ACT - *always* have a backup exam.

If you register for an exam, get your scores back, and see that they're high enough - awesome! Just cancel the next test and you're done. But if they aren't, you can roll right in. If you register for an exam, but realize that it's a bit too early, and you need to keep prepping - don't sweat it. Just cancel that test and register for a later one.

At this point, you know all about these tests, when they're offered, which ones to take, when to start prepping, where to register, and when you should walk in and take the real thing. But one last question remains: **how do you prepare for them?**

That's the subject of the next chapter. Fortunately, it's an easier answer than you might expect.

CHAPTER 13

How to Get High SAT and ACT Scores

n this chapter, I want to point out a few key lessons re: improving your SAT and ACT scores that you can take directly to the bank. The first is this:

There's no such thing as a "bad tester"

If you have low SAT or ACT scores, it means that *you're not good at taking the SAT or the ACT* - that is all. These tests are a specific mix of material and strategy which, when studied and applied consistently, become very easy to use. And, like every single skill and task on earth, taking these tests is something that you can get better at with *consistent practice* and the *proper guidance.*

Why do most people think that they're "bad testers?" They think they are bad testers because they either have *zero* experience prepping for these tests, or because they've prepped the wrong way. Saying that "you're a bad tester" is like saying that "you're bad at speaking German, because you don't speak it." That doesn't make any sense. You're not *bad at speaking German - you just don't speak German!* Once you learn how to, you'll be good at it!

The process of mastering the SAT/ACT is extremely similar to the process of learning a language. There are only three things that you need:

The Three Key Elements of Proper Test Prep

1. **Material knowledge.** If you're going to learn a new language, the *first* thing you need to learn is the vocabulary. If you want to conquer the SAT/ACT, you

need to learn the facts, formulas, and figures tested by these exams. This is your *foundation*. Without the key facts (math concepts, grammar rules, etc.) you can't use the strategies or answer the questions. *Anyone is capable of learning these facts.* You just need to study them in the right way to maximize your *retention* and your *ability to use them at will*.

However, if you memorize an entire German dictionary, it doesn't mean that you *speak* German. For that, we need the next element:

2. **Strategy and Tactics.** If you want to speak a language fluently, you need to understand the *grammar*. How do you use words, when, in what order, and how do they change depending on the situation? Similarly, you can't use SAT and ACT facts effectively unless you know the *strategies and tactics necessary for their use!* If you understand *how and why* these facts can be applied in different scenarios, and you understand how and when to fit them into different types of problems, you're going to be a fantastic test taker.

First comes material knowledge, then come strategy and tactics. The two are best when studied together, in concert. But even if you know all the vocabulary of a particular language, and understand the grammar, you're not considered *fluent* unless you have the third element:

3. **Realistic Application.** I took Italian for many years in school. I spent a summer in Rome. I know about 75% of the most common Italian vocab words, and about 75% of the grammar. Yet I am nowhere near speaking fluent Italian. Why not? *Because I never actually speak it.*

You can have all the math facts and strategies in the world, but if you never *use them* on a real SAT/ACT, on realistic problems, in realistic conditions, under realistic time constants, you're never going to get very good at *taking* the SAT/ACT.

Harnessing the power of realistic application is the final key in any proper test prep program. A great program will teach you the material you need to know, will show you the strategies and tactics required to use that material, and will force you to apply those material facts and strategic concepts to realistic, timed test material on a constant basis. If it's really good, it'll show you to use all three of these elements in concert, studying all of them at once, and using each element to enhance the other two.

If you combine all three elements into a test prep program, you're going to be in fantastic shape. Now the question becomes: *how do you find that program?*

How to Find a Proper Test Prep Program

Here, ladies and gentlemen, is where I need to degenerate into a quick bout of self-promotion. I've spent *thousands* of hours tutoring the SAT and ACT one-on-one, and thousands more crafting and refining my online program for both exams. I know what works and what doesn't, what order to teach it in, and exactly how to teach it.

Recently, I shut down my one-on-one tutoring practice even though I was charging **$1,000 an hour** for my services. I no longer take new students. The reason: I don't think one-on-one tutoring is nearly as effective as a simple, always-available program that allows you to study for a little bit a day, every day. Slow and steady wins the race. You can learn more about my decision here:

http://www.vox.com/2016/1/8/10728958/sat-tutor-expensive

Before I get into any specifics, let's look at the most common options you'll have when making this decision:

The Most Common SAT and ACT Prep Options:

1. **One-on-one tutoring.** This is often seen as the "gold standard" of test prep. But buyer beware: it's *extremely expensive* and *extremely inconsistent*. Not all tutors are created equal. I always recommend looking at online programs before hiring a tutor. If you need fine-tuning down the road, go for it. But it's wasteful to spend so much money on a tutor and sacrifice your own flexibility when there's so much that an effective online program can teach you.

    If you're hellbent on hiring a tutor, keep in mind that your tutor should be able to provide two things: **recommendations** and **results.** If you want to work with a tutor, get at least five references, and actually call them. This is a huge decision. Make sure you're working with someone whose clients have incredible things to say about him. And make sure that he keeps track of **results**. If someone boasts about how good he is, but doesn't show you what his effects are (or, worse yet, doesn't know what they are), then avoid him at all costs. **The only reason you're paying for a tutor is because a tutor can provide you with results.** If there's no track record...*beware.* Tutoring is inflexible and insanely expensive, so if you're going to go for it, at least make sure that you're getting the right tutor.

2. **Do not EVER sign up for classroom courses.** These have been shown, *countless times*, to have almost no effect on student performance. They're ineffective, overpriced, and inconvenient. Do not keep feeding this outdated industry. These classes are just a teacher reading a book in front of twenty people. Buy the book - don't pay for the class. The only reason classes are still around is because they're so ludicrously profitable. One teacher + twenty kids at a thousand dollars a head = plenty of money to go back into marketing and sales reps. **Avoid classroom courses like the plague.**

3. **Self-study.** If you want to try to do this on your own, it's going to be tough. These tests aren't like other academic subjects. They're weird and idiosyncratic, and it's extremely helpful to have a program or instructor that can guide you through this process. If you're already getting a really high score, and you just need to brush up on a few vocab words or math facts, you can probably do this on your own. But if you need to improve by more than about 100 points on the SAT, or 2-3 points on the ACT, you'll need some help.

4. **Online programs.** These are quickly eating up all the market share in the test prep space, and for very good reason: they're more effective and they're a better deal. That's why I've devoted my entire career to my own online program, at GreenTestPrep.com. While I can't speak for all the other programs out there, here's what I can say about my own:

    A) **It has crazy results.** The average student who uses GreenTestPrep.com improves by over 345 points on the SAT and over 4.66 points on the ACT. These point increases are *enormous* - enough to raise your application by entire college tiers. I recommend my program because *it works*, plain and simple.

B) **It allows you to start early and study on your own schedule.** The key to high scores is slow, consistent, steady prep. GreenTestPrep allows you to study for 15-30 minutes a day, whenever you want, wherever you happen to be. No tutor or classroom course can offer this, and most other online programs have set, inflexible schedules. The students who get the best results study on their own schedules, and fit their prep into any available slots they can find. They also realize that high school schedules are crazy and shift constantly, so flexibility is key.

C) **Cost and Guarantee.** My entire program costs a few hundred dollars and comes with an unconditional no-questions-asked guarantee.

D) **Complete adaptability.** I've spent years crafting a program which is both *standardized*, so that it can be delivered at large scale, and *adaptable*, so that anyone using it can get the best possible effect. As you work through my programs, you'll spend time on the things most important to *you*. Whether you're extremely advanced or extremely far behind, great at math and not so great at reading or vice versa, you'll learn and practice precisely what you need to in order to achieve the results you desire.

E) **Turnkey and holistic.** When you sign up for my programs, you don't need anything else. The programs combine all three elements of proper test prep, showing you how to conquer the material, strategies, and tactics necessary to beat these exams, and pushing you through a rigorous application program to enhance your skills. I'm confident that *anyone* who tries my programs will see huge results.

If you have any questions about either program, don't hesitate to get in touch at https://greentestprep.com/contact-us/ - We'll be happy to assist! **Also, remember that you can use the code "WYGRcode" at checkout for $25 off the entire program.**

No matter which option you choose, GET STARTED!

Remember: the ideal time to start prepping is *freshman year*. Once that point hits, *the clock is ticking!* The earlier you start, the easier, more relaxing, and more productive this entire process will be.

Getting great SAT and ACT scores isn't *easy*, but it's extremely *doable*. If you get the right instruction and put in the work, you'll see remarkable results. I've raised students' SAT scores by over 900 points and ACT scores by 15. But there are two things that these high achievers have all had in common:

1. **They put in the work**
2. **They started early**

This isn't something you can knock out last-minute. Before you go on to the next chapter, make SAT/ACT preparations *now.* You'll thank me later!

CHAPTER 14

SAT Subject Tests

f you're like most people, you're not too concerned about the SAT Subject Tests. They seem like pesky little annoyances that don't matter much...until the day comes when you realize that *most competitive colleges require two of them*, and you need to take them in three weeks or your application won't be accepted.

Fortunately, there's nothing *difficult* about these tests. But you need to think about them as far in advance as possible. They can be an incredibly important part of your overall application, and you don't want to end up with sub-par scores when high scores are so easy to attain.

If you plan in advance and know the purpose that these tests serve, you'll have a much easier time getting into your target schools. First, let's figure out **what they are** and **why you have to take them.**

What's the Point of the SAT Subject Tests?

The SAT Subject Tests are an important part of your college application strategy – but they're very different from the SAT 1 and the ACT. As I already told you, the SAT 1 and the ACT are *eliminators* – in other words, they don't *get you into* your target schools – they simply get your application opened or rejected on the spot. If your scores are *high enough*, administrators will look at your real application – your extra-curriculars, recommendations, essays, etc. – if they're not, your application will get tossed in the trash.

The SAT Subject Tests are quite different. Your SAT Subject Test scores don't show up in round one – they show up in round two, as *part of who you are.*

So while the SAT 1 and ACT can get you *rejected* from great schools, but very rarely *accepted,* the SAT Subject Tests can't get you *rejected* from great schools, but *they can help you to get accepted.* They're last-minute comparative tools that administrators use when all else fails.

The SAT 1 and ACT tell colleges that you have the raw ability necessary to master their coursework. If your scores are high enough, it gives them a base level of confidence that you can "hack it" – from there, they'll see who you really are.

The SAT Subject Tests, on the other hand, tell schools *WHAT you're really good at.* As you'll learn in the next section of this book, getting into college is all about crafting a narrative. "You should let me in because I'm an incredible _____." What's in that blank doesn't matter so as long *something* is there, and so long as *you focus relentlessly on telling that story.*

Are you a great writer? Mathematician? Scientist? Humanitarian? So long as you're a great *something,* colleges will take note. If you have nothing in particular going for you, you'll get chopped.

Your SAT Subject Tests are a great way to add credibility to your story. If you say you're a great scientist, high SAT chemistry and physics scores will prove your story. If you say that you're a great writer, you should have high SAT literature and language scores. The SAT Subject Tests are *numerical proof* of the story that you're trying to tell to colleges.

Getting a 500/800 on the bio SAT won't necessarily get you *rejected* from a great school if the rest of your application is strong – but if you're saying that you want to be a marine biologist, a 750/800 will certainly help to keep you out of the "liar pile."

Think of the SAT Subject Tests as the mortar in between your application's bricks – it holds everything in place and provides proof and structure for admissions officers.

Which colleges require SAT Subject Tests, and which ones do they require?

The majority of the most competitive colleges require SAT Subject Tests, and even the schools that don't *require* these tests still take them seriously as a way to verify your overall narrative.

HOWEVER, every school is different. Some schools don't require them at all. Some require *any* two. Some require two specific Subject Tests. Some require one "humanities" test, and one "math or science" test. It all depends on the school.

It's your job to figure out which Subject Tests your target schools require so that you can plan as far in advance as possible. Remember when I had you put together your list of target colleges? There's a reason why we *started* with that process. It's essential that you know the particular requirements of every college you're applying to.

How to Find Out Which SAT Subject Tests Your Schools Require:

There are four ways in which your target schools can treat the SAT Subject Tests:

1. **Two are REQUIRED**
2. **Two are required, but you can submit an ACT score instead**
3. **They are *considered*, but not *required***
4. **They aren't even considered**

In general, the more competitive the school, the more intense the SAT Subject Test requirements happen to be.

To find out the requirements of your schools, just Google every school on your list like so:

"SAT Subject Test Requirements for [school in question]."

You'll find their requirements listed clearly on their website. If they aren't listed clearly, you can also use the College Board search tool here:

https://bigfuture.collegeboard.org/college-search

If you type in the name of the college, go to that school's page, click "applying" on the left, and then click "application requirements" in the menu at the bottom, you'll find out your target schools' requirements.

That's all there is to it. However, before we move on, there's something you need to know:

Whether or not you are *required* to take the SAT Subject Test isn't very relevant – these exams are probably THE best way to demonstrably prove your expertise. If you don't take them, you'll be compared to countless students who will – and you're losing a valuable opportunity to separate yourself from the pack.

If you want to be a doctor, and that's what you're telling to colleges, you should *really* consider studying for and taking the Biology SAT Subject Test. Even if your dream school doesn't *require* it, don't you want to do everything you can to show them that you care passionately about your area of interest, and to demonstrate your expertise?

If you're applying to be a math major, and you don't take a math SAT Subject Test... it just looks weird.

Even if there's no particular subject you're "showing off," taking a few SAT Subject Tests and getting incredible grades shows that you're "Ivy Caliber." Most of the nation's most competitive schools require SAT Subject Tests - many of the less competitive schools don't. If you show other schools that you can get 700+ scores on tests they don't even require – *they notice, even if they say they don't.*

***Quick Note: many schools allow you to switch out AP grades for SAT Subject Test scores. Again, to find out which ones allow this, use Google or call the schools on your list and find out. As far as I'm concerned, high AP scores perform the same function as

great SAT Subject Test scores – they show that you're an expert within a given field. If a school accepts either test interchangeably, then both accomplish the same feat. Find out as soon as possible. We'll cover the AP exams later on in this book.

At this point, you should have a pretty darn good idea of whether or not you need to take the SAT Subject Tests or not (hint: you probably should).

Now it's time to figure out *when* you should take these tests, and which ones you should take:

When to Take the Subject Tests (and Which Ones to Take)

If you're reading this, it means that you've decided to take the SAT Subject Tests. Good call! High scores on your SAT Subject Tests show colleges that you mean business and are willing to go the extra mile.

Getting great SAT Subject Test scores boils down to three factors:

1. **Picking the right time to take them (and planning as far in advance as possible)**
2. **Taking the right ones**
3. **Studying for them effectively**

WHEN SHOULD YOU TAKE YOUR SAT SUBJECT TEST?

SAT Subject Tests are given on the same days and times as the SAT 1 (with a few exceptions). That means that you can't take Subject Tests and the SAT 1 on the same day. However, you can take *up to three SAT Subject Tests on the same day*. I don't recommend it, but it's good to know that you can.

You can find a full menu of all the SAT Subject Tests, along with the dates when they're offered, here:

http://professionals.collegeboard.com/testing/sat-subject/register/
test-dates

While these dates are only a few months in advance, the tests are usually offered at or around the same times every year, so if you're planning for next year, you can assume that these dates are pretty much static.

As far as *which date* you should pick, I offer two pieces of advice:

1. **Get them out of the way as early as possible.** The SAT Subject Tests aren't something to be left until the last minute.
    If you have absolutely terrible SAT Subject Test scores, most colleges won't eliminate you from the applicant pool – but if your scores are awesome, they'll help to put you in a league of your own. Therefore, you should give yourself plenty of time to achieve high Subject Test scores and add some paprika to your application.

    While I don't recommend taking these tests more than once, it's still good to give yourself the opportunity to do so. If you bomb your only shot at the SAT Subject Test...well, that's that. If you get a sub-par score early on, you can shoot for a higher score at a later date.

    Start planning for your SAT Subject Tests *today*. If you can get them out of the way, and give yourself plenty of time to achieve high scores, you'll be at a distinct advantage. Don't leave this chapter with a vague idea of when these tests will happen. Look at your calendar - look at the classes you're taking - look at your plan for the SAT/ACT, and then figure out when you're taking your Subject Tests.

    This leads to the next big question: which Subject Tests should you take, and *when's the best possible time to take them?*

2. **Take Subject Tests in areas where you're already strong, or right after you've taken that subject in school!** In other words, if you've just finished a chemistry class, and you did well, try taking the Chemistry Subject Test right away!
    Remember: bad Subject Test scores won't really hurt you, but great scores will certainly help. It's much better to get high scores in "less impressive" subjects than it is to get mediocre scores in "fancier" subjects.

    A few 700+ scores on multiple Subject Tests show that you're *really good at stuff*. And as obvious as this sounds, *colleges like students who are good at stuff.* So take the tests that give you the best chances of attaining high scores, regardless of what those tests happen to be.

TAKE THE RIGHT TESTS

When it comes to the tests themselves, the Subject Tests are NOTHING like the SAT 1 or ACT. The SAT 1 and ACT are all about strategy, approach, and familiarity. My students improve their SAT 1 and ACT scores by so much because they figure out the *tests themselves* - not just the material within them. The material is easy – the strategy, tactics, and approach/application requirements of these tests are extremely complicated.

The SAT Subject Tests are the exact opposite. They involve no real strategy and no real "approach" – most of the time, you either know the material or you don't. Your score is a pure function of whether or not you know the facts required by the tests – there's nothing else to them.

Of course, you still need strong multiple-choice test taking skills if you want the best scores possible. But if you've learned how to take a standardized test the right way (something I focus on heavily in my own programs), this won't be a problem. Overall, they're just simple tests of material.

And unlike the SAT 1 and ACT, which appeal to two different *styles* of student and learner, these tests are best suited to students who *know certain stuff.*

Are you good at French? Take the French Language Subject Test. Good at chemistry? Take the chemistry one. Good at math? You get the idea.

When you've just finished a particular class (especially an AP class), it's the perfect time to take the Subject Test on that subject, since your schoolwork will have already killed a lot of your study birds with one stone. And we hate birds around here.

Plan in advance and take your subject-specific tests as soon as possible after you're finished taking classes that have to do with them. Also, for extra bonus points, study Subject Test material DURING your class and you'll end up getting much better grades along with a better Subject Test scores (talk about killing a lot of birds...).

Two other rules to go by:

1. **If you're really awesome at something, take that SAT Subject Test.** This goes without saying. If you're freakishly good at chemistry, or fluent in Spanish, etc., take the test that corresponds. Why wouldn't you?

2. **If you're trying to show off a certain skill or aptitude, take the Subject Test(s) that match up.** If you're trying to show that you're a great writer, take the Literature test. If you're trying to show that you want to be a NASA scientist, take Math 2C and Physics. We'll get into your "narrative" in the next section, but just know this: if you're going to say that you're great at something, you'll want as much proof as possible. These test provide fantastic proof.

Still stuck?

If you still have no clue which SAT Subject Tests you want to take, I'd recommend:

1. Math 1C
   And
2. US or World History

Most schools require a Math Subject Test anyhow, so take the easiest one (there's a 1c and a 2c, and the 2c is significantly harder). Most schools also require a "humanities" Subject Test – the history exams are the easiest of these. They just require a lot of factual information – if you study them consistently, you'll remember them, and you'll do well. Done and done. There's not a human being alive who can't do well on either of these exams – all you need is a memory and a bit of hard work.

Now that you know which tests to take and when to take them, it's time to figure out how to study for them.

How to Study for the SAT Subject Tests

I have great news: studying for these tests exactly like studying for pretty much any exam that you take in school. They're all about material knowledge, and that's about it. There's almost zero strategy on any of these tests (with the exception of the Literature exam, which requires the same strategies required for the SAT 1 Critical Reading section that I teach in my online SAT system at https://greentestprep.com).

Getting a great Subject Test score is all about knowing the material on the test and then studying the living bejeezus out of it.

The real trick is in studying the *right* material to improve your chances of getting a great score.

Before we continue, know this:

You should be able to predict your Subject Test scores within 10 points of your actual scores before you ever walk into the testing center. There are *no surprises on these exams.*

As I said earlier in this section, the SAT 1 and ACT both have a lot of variables at play – strategy, tricky wording, insane section formatting, ludicrous timing requirements, etc. etc. The Subject Tests do not. At all. You know your stuff or you don't, and that's honestly all there is to it.

If you want great scores on these tests, you just need to follow these two steps:

1. **Find the right materials to study.**
2. **Study these materials until you have them memorized.**

Time to get reading! Here is a book that I highly recommend to anyone studying for their Subject Tests:

College Board Official SAT Subject Test Guide
This is the official manual – buy it no matter what you're taking, and read through the whole thing. It'll give you a ton of insights into these tests, their construction, and what you need to study.

Also, if you're still not sure which one you want to take, this is a perfect way to "shop around" and see what works best. You'll get a quick glimpse of each Subject Test, which should make it easy to figure out which one is right for you (i.e. which one seems easiest to you).

By the way, as a reminder: the best Subject Tests to take are always the ones that will give you the highest possible scores. There's no point in taking these exams unless you're going to do well, so set the odds in your favor and pick the right ones.

Once you pick the tests that you want to take, you'll need to get some good study materials. Rather than give you a list of books for each test, I'm going to give you a much simpler recommendation:

1. **Go to Amazon.com.**
2. **Search "{subject in question} subject test."**
3. **Buy the books with the best reviews.**

Some brands make *amazing* math Subject Test books and *garbage* US History books, and vice versa, and things change rapidly from year to year.

More material is better than less material, so just get your hands on everything you possibly can that has good reviews and start studying like a maniac.

Once you have the materials in hand, there's one last thing you need to learn:

How to Study Effectively for SAT Subject Tests:

All of these tests are completely different, and test very specific materials. I can't give you French language tips, literature tips, and Math 2C tips in one chapter, so instead, I'm going to boil down this entire process to 4 steps:

1. **Find out what you DON'T know.**
   As soon as you can, take a practice test and figure out everything that seems weird or unfamiliar. Circle it, document it, and make a flashcard out of it.

   These tests do *one* thing: check your knowledge of certain facts and formulas. You know them or you don't. The first thing you need to do is find out what you don't know.

2. **Read through the books, work through as many questions as you can, and use answer explanations to help you make sense of the ones you get wrong.**

If you're not sure how to conjugate a certain word in Spanish, use your books' answer explanations to guide you to the light.

You can also use the internet to find these facts. Again, this isn't rocket science – these are just facts. Google "how to conjugate X in French" and you'll find it. *There isn't a single fact on these tests that can't simply be Googled.* The material is public access, and the strategy is non-existent.

3. **Use your TEACHERS to help you.**
   I want to point one awesome thing out:

   The SAT 1 is a freakishly precise exam that needs to be taught by people familiar with the SAT 1. However, SAT Subject Tests can be taught by any teacher familiar with the subject material!

   Having trouble with a certain chemistry concept? Ask your chemistry teacher. Can't deal with a certain French verb tense? Ask your French teacher! Your school's teachers are a huge resource in your mission to get great Subject Test scores. Use them.

4. **Practice, practice, practice.** Did you think there'd be some magical way of getting better scores? Unfortunately, there isn't.
   Find out what you don't know. Then learn it.

   I refuse to tutor SAT Subject Tests. Why? *Because these exams are way too simple to justify my hourly rate!* My knowledge of the SAT 1 and ACT are worth the price – I know these complex tests inside and out, and I have a unique ability to enhance my students' scores. But *anybody* can teach the SAT Subject Tests – all the knowledge within is common knowledge. If you want a tutor, you'd be just as well off hiring a freshman college student as you would be hiring me.

   These tests are just like any other exam that tests your ability to regurgitate information; if you have it ready to regurgitate, you can do it. If not, you're cooked like a turkey.

   Every day, just set aside *20 minutes* and study your face off.

Remember: *consistency is more important than quantity!* Don't put this stuff off, then study for 16 hours the day before your test. Spread your prep out over the long term for better results and a more relaxing experience.

To summarize:

1. **Find out what you don't know.**
2. **Find out how to know it.**
3. **Study it repeatedly and consistently until test day.**

That's all there is to it! You know *when* to take your SAT Subject Tests, you know *if you need to take them in the first place*, you know *which materials you need to study*, and you know *how to study them.*

Now get to it! Look at your calendar, figure out when you'll be able to knock two of these things out, put the registration dates in your calendar, and start studying like a maniac.

CHAPTER 15

Learning Disabilities, Extra Time, and Special Accommodations

Before we move on to the next section, there's one more important issue we need to address: special accommodations, extra time, and learning disabilities.

If you don't have any learning disabilities, and don't need any special accommodations, skip this chapter. If you do, this chapter is an absolute must.

If you have a learning disability, psychological disorder, or physical disability (or suspect that you do), you should get extra time and accommodations. This isn't a recommendation; it's a requirement. If you don't have any of the above conditions, then move on - this chapter isn't for you.

The SAT and ACT have nothing to do with your intelligence - they simply test how good you are at taking the SAT/ACT. But these tests are almost custom-tailored to be difficult for students with learning disabilities, which is part of the reason why they get their bad reputations. If you have *any* learning disability or physical impairment, you should apply for extra time and accommodations to level the playing field.

Before we get into the details, there are two things you need to know:

1. **College admissions committees will not know that you received extra time/ accommodations.** Due to the Americans With Disabilities Act, they

are prohibited from knowing or asking. So, on a college admissions level, there is only upside, no downside.

2. **There is nothing wrong with getting extra time.** I can't tell you how many parents I've spoken to who think that there's something "dishonest" about getting their children extra time. Nothing could be further from the truth. Let me state it as simply as possible:

   If you DO NOT HAVE learning, psychological, or physical disabilities, and you apply for special accommodations, it's despicable. But if you DO have any of these things, it is irresponsible, unfair, and foolish for you NOT to get extra accommodations.

The SAT/ACT, "un-leveled," are very hard for students with learning disabilities. Let me share two quick stories with you to emphasize how important it is that you seek the appropriate level of assistance:

A) I once taught a student with moderate to severe dyslexia. He was incredibly bright - he understood difficult concepts in seconds, had incredible logical reasoning abilities, and developed a fantastic vocabulary. But his on-page reading skills suffered due to his disability. In short, it took him a while to read passages. His mother, fearing that she would make him feel "handicapped" if she asked for special accommodations, refused to get him extra time and other help for his dyslexia. As a result, he scored a 310 on his Critical Reading section. Out of 800. Do you think he felt handicapped?

His father, taking matters into his own hands, went through hell and high water at the last minute, under incredible time pressure, to get him the special accommodations he needed. When he took the test again, months later, he scored a 680 on his Critical Reading section. But for the months leading up to his 680, I've never dealt with a more discouraged or heartbroken student in my entire career.

B) I once worked with a girl who had very bad ADHD. Smart as a whip, creative, perceptive, but she couldn't sit still. She would drift, and as a result, it took her longer than most of my students to complete the sections that didn't engage her. She was interested in math, and hence her math scores were high and she always finished on time. But she hated grammar, and thus her Writing scores were very low. When I worked with her during sessions, and we spent 40-45 minutes on a Writing section, she could get 33/35 questions right. But when she was under time pressure, on her own, she'd only be able to complete about half the problems before time ran out.

This story doesn't have the happy ending that the first one did. Her mother and father refused to believe that she had ADHD, although it was clear from her behavior and academic performance that she did (in case you're wondering, one of the clearest signs of ADD is incredibly high grades in the areas in which your student is interested, and abysmal grades in the areas in which she is not). No extra time, no special accommodations, nothing. So while I brought her math score from a 620 to a 750, her Writing score went from a 470 to a 510. Not awful, but she had the capacity to do far better than she did.

It is your duty to get as many advantages as you possibly can.

With that in mind, let's go over which disabilities qualify, what types of extra help you can get, how you can diagnose these issues, and how to apply for special accommodations.

What types of special help and accommodations can you get?

You can find a very comprehensive list of all special accommodations on the College Board website using the following link:

https://www.collegeboard.org/students-with-disabilities/typical-accommodations

And on the ACT website using the following link:

http://www.actstudent.org/regist/disab/

The most common types of special accommodations include, but are not limited to:

- Extended time, which adds 50% to 100% of the time usually given for these tests
- Computer usage, for students who have trouble writing

- Accommodations for students with reading impairments and disabilities, including someone to read the tests out loud for them
- Accommodations for students with hearing impairments, such as someone to give them test directions in sign language
- Extra and extended breaks
- Special testing spaces, such as private rooms for students with severe ADHD, or screens to block out distractions

There are many more accommodations than these, but the above list represents the vast majority of what most people request.

What types of disabilities qualify for extra time and special accommodations?

Learning disabilities, physical disabilities, and psychiatric disabilities of all kinds qualify for special accommodations.

To figure out if you're eligible, use this page for the SAT:

https://www.collegeboard.org/students-with-disabilities/eligibility

And this page for the ACT:

http://www.act.org/aap/pdf/ACT-Policy-for-Documentation.pdf

Who can help to simplify the process?

Almost all schools, public and private, have a *Services for Students with Disabilities* department. You should talk to your *SSD Coordinator* as soon as possible to set up a meeting and figure out whether or not you qualify. Online forms are great, but speaking to a trained, professional expert is much better.

GET STARTED NOW. NOT TOMORROW, BUT NOW.

If you want to get special accommodations, you need to do so as early as imaginably possible. While the deadline for special accommodations is technically only four weeks from the test date, the process takes much longer than that because **documentation is everything.**

If you don't have your disabilities documented, you will not be able to get these special accommodations. And setting up appointments, running tests, and getting results takes a lot of time. To document these disabilities, you'll need to follow the following processes for the SAT:

http://www.collegeboard.com/ssd/student/index.html#documentation

And these for the ACT:

http://www.actstudent.org/regist/disab/policy.html

The first step in getting accommodations for any disorder is documenting the disorder in an official context. You should get started with this process immediately.

How do I actually apply for the extra accommodations?
You do that here for the SAT:

http://www.collegeboard.com/ssd/student/index.html#apply

And here for the ACT:

http://www.actstudent.org/regist/disab/

The easiest way to do is through your school's *SSD Coordinator*. This is a process that *can* be done on your own, but you should get help. It's much easier to navigate these waters when you have a professional on your side.

Final Note:
Between the websites I've provided and your school's *Services for Students With Disabilities Coordinator*, you should have everything you need to get extra accommodations – if you deserve them. I just want to make it clear once again that these special accommodations are not a "cop out," nor are they "unfair." They're just a way of leveling the playing field and of making sure that you have the most opportunities possible for your future.

If you feel strange about these accommodations, remember that you *are entitled to receive them*. The SAT/ACT aren't intelligence or aptitude tests - they're bizarre, hyper-specific exams that only test one thing: how good you are at taking them. Special accommodations make you better at taking them, so why not?

Before you begin any sort of SAT or ACT prep program, I highly recommend that you start this process. If you don't know whether or not you'll have extra time, it's impossible to give yourself the proper amount of time when you take practice tests or to work through practice problems under the appropriate amount of time pressure. Figure out, as soon as possible, whether you'll be getting extra time - if you are, practice with extended time in place.

Section Four: You

Or: what happens when you avoid the chopping block and colleges
start to wonder who you really are as a person

CHAPTER 16

The Robes Are Off - Now What?

Congratulations! You've maintained a high GPA, you've gotten good SAT or ACT scores, and you've survived round two. Unlike the countless students whose applications were tossed in the rejection pile, your application is now breathing rarified air - you've made it to round three.

There's only one problem: *you still need to avoid getting rejected!*

At this point, the admissions officers have done everything in their power to cut the fat and reduce their options. They've let the red carpet vouchers sneak by, and they've eliminated everyone with crappy grades and sub-standard test scores. But *they still have work to do.* And, unfortunately for most applicants, their work involves *throwing a majority of the remaining applications in the garbage.*

There's an often-quoted "fact" that says that Harvard could let in six classes full of valedictorians with perfect SAT scores. This is a ludicrous exaggeration, but the *idea* behind this statement is quite accurate. Harvard, and every other competitive college in the land, has *way more than enough applicants with amazing grades and test scores.* But, as you might have guessed, they don't just let in the kids with 4.38 weighted GPAs, and cut the kids with 4.37s.

Why not? Why don't they just let in the people with the absolute best metrics and cut everyone else?

Fantastic metrics don't GET YOU INTO colleges - they just PREVENT YOU FROM GETTING REJECTED. Once you've made the cut, you need to prove that you are A CONTRIBUTING, PASSIONATE HUMAN BEING.

Let's quickly return to the dating analogy. Let's say that you start talking to someone who you feel is very attractive. At this point, you're trying to get to know them, figure out their personality, and, if you get along, start dating them. You're NOT looking for someone 1% more physically attractive, regardless of her personality. Once your date is *attractive enough for you*, you then focus solely on her personality traits.

Colleges are the same way. Sure, they could just accept the kids with the absolute best test scores and GPAs - but they'd end up with a class full of duds. They need to find people who are **interesting, interested**, and who **have demonstrated a passion for SOMETHING in life.** What that *something* is doesn't really matter. But if it's not there at all, you're in big trouble.

Do *not* think that you're out of the woods if your grades and scores are high. That's just the bare minimum. High grades and scores keep colleges interested enough to find out who you really are. So the question becomes this: **who do colleges actually want you to be? What kind of person are they looking for?** To answer that, we'll move on to the next chapter.

CHAPTER 17

The Myth of the Well-Rounded Student

f you talk to a lot of parents about college, you'll end up hearing the same phrase used over and over again: the "well-rounded student." The vast majority of people believe that colleges are looking for "well-rounded kids." In fact, nothing could be further from the truth.

Colleges ARE NOT looking for well-rounded STUDENTS - they are looking for well-rounded CLASSES.

Can you imagine what would happen if Harvard let in thousands of kids who were sort of good at twenty tasks each? What would they end up with? A giant class full of mediocre hobbyists who never committed to anything, flittered their attention away on countless random tasks, and never actually did anything of note.

Colleges don't want "Jacks of All Trades" - they want an enormous collection of people who are each absolutely *amazing* at *something*.

They want a few kids who are incredible basketball players. A few mind-blowing musicians. A few world-class scientists. A few potential Pulitzer Prize winners. A few actors who'll end up winning Oscars. A few mathematicians who'll revolutionize the field. The list goes on.

The romanticized version of the "renaissance man" applicant is total and utter BS. Colleges want people who are really good at ONE thing. The CLASS, as a whole, will be a renaissance class.

Every freshman class is composed of hundreds/thousands of students. Together, they can make up a wildly diverse group of experts, all of whom are capable of accomplishing something remarkable. Harvard isn't just known for its great writers, or mathematicians, or scientists - it's known for its great *everything*. But very few of Harvard's students are *all of those things*. Each of them is just amazing at *one* of those things. Harvard then has the chance to sharpen their skills and send them out into the world to make money and build reputations.

Being good at lots of stuff is *icing on the cake*. For instance, I spoke with a kid the other day who was a world-class soccer player, and who was being recruited by some of the best colleges in the country. He *also* happened to have an aviation license, was the best debater on his debate club, and was class president. That is *extremely* impressive. But it's only impressive because *he is really awesome at something, has good grades and scores, and yet STILL manages to be awesome at other stuff, too.* If he was a JV soccer player who spent an hour a week in debate, was trying to get his pilot's license, and ran for class president...no one would be impressed. **Mastery in ONE domain must come first.** Before we move on to the next chapter, which discusses the formation of your mastery, there's another reason why I need to dispel this myth: **the idea of the well-rounded student blinds you to the needs of colleges.**

If every college were looking for a "round" kid, then every college would want the same kind of applicant. This is blatantly not the case.

Every college has specific "holes" in its roster that it's desperately trying to fill, and other "overflows" that it's trying to get rid of. These holes are usually reputational in nature. For instance, MIT has long been known as sort of a "nerd school," full of mathematicians and scientists, but lacking "creative types." So a few years ago, they started actively making a push for more "humanities-focused" students to round things out. They hired world-class English and history professors. They pumped more energy into their humanities departments. *If you were a "humanities-strong applicant" during that time period, and* <u>*you knew that MIT was looking for your kind of application*</u>*, you would have had a much easier time getting in!*

If you're awesome at football, but not *that* awesome - *don't* focus on Alabama, where you'll probably be the worst player on the team - find a really good school with a struggling football team, which has a coach desperately looking for good players but coming short on recruits, and apply there.

All colleges have *too many experts* filling certain holes, and *not enough experts* filling others. If you know which experts they're looking for, and which experts they have too many of, you'll end up barking up the right tree.

Colleges don't want well-rounded students. With that in mind, you need to become *sharp*.

CHAPTER 18

The Big Blank and Your ONE Thing

t's time for a quick review. Colleges want two things: money and better reputations, both of which support each other.

Here's how they get money:

- Tuition
- Donations
- Peripheral Sources

Here's how they get **better reputations:**

- Having really amazing graduates who go on to do lots of awesome stuff
- Having graduates who make a ton of money
- Having students who do really awesome stuff while they're at the school

These are simplified lists, but they're pretty comprehensive. If a college has ludicrously wealthy, world-famous graduates who do all sorts of glorious, world-class stuff while they're on campus, that college is going to be pretty well regarded.

This means that more people will apply to the college with higher metrics, which means that more people who probably have more money are going to apply (more tuition). The rich graduates will donate more when they graduate (more donations) and others will be tempted to donate more in an attempt to get their kid in (more donations). Their kids will do lots of awesome stuff on campus, such as win lots of sports games, which will attract TV networks who will share ad revenues (peripheral revenues), and attract brilliant researchers and teachers who will discover patents and write amazing papers which will make the school even more money (peripherals again) and enhance its reputation even further.

The cycle goes on and on. So what's the weakest link in this chain? What do colleges absolutely *need* in order to keep this cycle going? **People who are awesome at stuff.**

I know this might seem obvious and sound childish, but it's the most honest and straightforward way to put it: **colleges only want applicants who are really, really good at SOMETHING.**

WHAT thing? ANY thing!!!

If you want to avoid getting chopped by a member of the admissions committee, there's a blank that you need to fill:

The Most Important Blank in the World:
You should let me in because I am an ABSOLUTELY AMAZING _____.

What's in that blank?
Writer? Quarterback? Scientist? Author? Leader? Philanthropist? Robotics expert? Chef? Architect? Painter? Guitarist? Tennis player? Director? Graphic designer? Audio engineer? Watchmaker? Interior designer? Entrepreneur? Investor? Problem solver?

I really can't emphasize this point enough: *it doesn't matter WHAT you're amazing at so long as you've demonstrated* **the capacity to develop excellence in SOMETHING.**

This is the entire key. It's not that colleges believe that a great 17-year-old poet is going to go on to become the Poet Laureate of the United States - they simply believe that *any 17-year-old that has the capacity to get awesome at SOMETHING will end up doing SOMETHING noteworthy with his or her life.*

People who get really good at things tend to get even better, or to get really good at even more things.

When kids attain a level of excellence in any field, it says that they're *focused, driven, talented,* and *willing to put in the work necessary to attain success.* They know how much work it takes to become a master of their craft. They know how to tackle obstacles, shrug off defeat, and keep pushing forward. But that's not all - high school kids who are awesome at *something* aren't just *interesting - they're also* <u>interested</u>.

The people who become the most INTERESTING are the people who are most INTERESTED.

If you want to be good at something, you have to be interested in it.

Nothing is funnier to me than parents who try to "force" their kids to be good at something. The kid can't *stand* baseball, yet their dad wants him to be the next Babe Ruth. The kid *begs* not to go to piano practice, yet the mom wants her to end up at Carnegie Hall. *It will NEVER happen.*

Recently, I read a funny story about Tiger Woods. When he was a little kid, he started coming home with bags full of nickels. His dad asked him where he was getting the money, and found out that he was putting for nickels with other members at the golf club. His dad forbade him from ever playing for nickels again. So the next day, Tiger came home with a big bag full of quarters...

I got a huge kick out of this story because it illustrates an obvious point that many people forget: *if you want to be really good at something, you need to be into it.* Mastery, before anything else, requires *attention.* And attention isn't something that can be *asked* for or *forced* - it only comes from within. There are plenty of world-class race car drivers, billionaires, and best-selling authors who practically flunked out of school, were diagnosed with ADD, and were generally seen as "unpromising" - yet they were able to pay attention to *one* thing that *interested them,* and boom - they were off to the races.

If you're interested in soccer now, you might not be interested in soccer when you graduate college - but that's not what colleges care about. Colleges simply want to see someone who *has the capacity for interest.* If you can get interested in *something,* then you'll *always* be interested in *something.* That's what they want to see.

To colleges, there is no bigger red flag than a student who has no interests.

No one is less appealing than a student with bad grades, bad scores, and no extracurriculars whatsoever. What's in it for the college? No evidence of work ethic, no evidence of interest or passion - what are you offering them, exactly?

But even if you have good grades and good test scores, colleges aren't going to be very impressed if you have *nothing that interests you.* We've all heard the phrase: "if you're bored then you're boring." You should also know this one: "if you're interested, you're interesting." Kids with good grades, good scores, and no extracurriculars are like models who, when asked what they're into, respond: "like, being good looking?" Only the shallowest of colleges are going to be interested.

To show colleges that you're *interested,* you have to do three things:

1. **Find something that you're ACTUALLY interested in.** Colleges can smell a fake from a mile away (and if you're not actually into something, it's hard to believe that you'll become very good at it).
2. **Pursue it to the point of excellence and *try* to rack up *accomplishments* in that domain.**
3. **Make sure that those pursuits and accomplishments are TANGIBLE.**

The third item is the most important of all. Remember: colleges are brilliant at sniffing out liars and truth stretchers. Admissions officers can spot a "fake enthusiast" from a mile away (which is a big subject in the next chapter). Therefore, no matter which expertise you pick, you need to make sure that it is in some way *documentable.*

The Fake Writer

A colleague of mine shared a story that perfectly exemplifies the problem with many "un-interested" applicants. A client of his had zero extracurricular activities to speak of, and was applying to a school known for its competitive writing program. The student had fantastic English scores and good SAT Writing and Critical Reading grades, and, though he didn't have any *documented* writing activities to speak of, he offered this up as a potential element of his application: "I read all the time, and I've helped a bunch of friends with their papers."

Do you see the problem here? He failed all three requirements.

1. **The student SAID he was interested in writing, but hadn't actually written anything.** If you "think you want to do something," you're not actually that into it. Sure, you might like the *idea* of being a writer, but *if you don't write, then you are NOT A WRITER.*
2. **The student hadn't pursued that interest and hadn't racked up a single accomplishment in the domain of writing.**
3. **The accomplishments that he *did* reference were totally intangible.** There's no way to prove that you've read a lot. There's no way to show colleges that you've edited your friends' essays.

   I'm not saying this kid was a bad person - I am saying that he was a bad applicant. So how could he have done things right?

How to Demonstrate Your Expertise

It's not enough to just *say* that you're great at something - you need to *prove* that you're great at something. Colleges aren't going to take your word for it. **Once you pick your area of interest, you need to do EVERYTHING POSSIBLE to document and demonstrate that interest.**

If you're into writing, that's fantastic. Here are some things you can do to prove it to colleges:

- Write for the school newspaper and get as many articles published as possible
- Win a leadership position in your school newspaper, literary magazine, etc.
- Submit your writing to contests and major publications and try to get published for real, win awards, etc. You don't need to be in *The New Yorker* or win a Pulitzer; getting published in *any* real publication and winning any prize is impressive (and documented)
- Start a creative writing club at your school (or attain a leadership position in one)

- Make sure you get awesome English grades
- Attend a college writing program over the summer
- Take one or both AP English classes and exams and get good grades
- Take the Literature SAT Subject test and rock it
- Do *anything possible* that shows how much you love writing, how much better you want to get at writing, and how good you are at writing.

The great thing is, if you're *actually* interested in writing, then finding ways to prove your interest will be darn easy. You'll be *living the life of an interested writer,* so the rest will take care of itself.

Recently, an aspiring applicant who came to GreenTestPrep.com asked me the following question:

"I want to show colleges that I'm into robotics. How do I show them that?"

My answer to him was very straightforward: *How the heck would I know!?* I don't know anything about robots. *You're* the one who's into robots - so shouldn't *you* know how to prove it? If you were truly interested, you'd be *attending robotics programs and classes, building robots, entering robotics competitions, submitting models for robotic designs, etc.* YOU are the expert! YOU are the one who's interested. YOU are the one who needs to know the answers to these questions!

Some areas of interest are much easier to demonstrate than others. For instance, if you're really into soccer, you just need to be a good soccer player. Your coach will do the vouching for you. Others require a bit more creativity, but if you're actually interested, it won't be tough to prove.

What if I can't fill the blank? What if I'm just not that interested in anything?

You probably won't get into a rally competitive school. I'm not trying to be a jerk - I'm just being honest. If you have no extracurricular interests, and nothing going for you outside of your grades and test scores, then the only schools interested in your application will be the schools that need to raise their average GPAs and test scores. Is it *impossible* that a kid with a 4.1 average and a 2200 SAT with no extracurriculars will get into Columbia or Princeton? No. It happens. But it's going to be really hard.

If you're applying to a not-so-competitive college, and you have great scores and grades, you don't really need awesome extracurriculars. It's your awesome grades vs. everyone else's mediocre grades, which automatically sets you apart from the pack. But when you're applying to a competitive college, where *everyone* who makes it past round two has high grades and scores, your lack of extracurriculars is going to be a major blow.

If you already have an area of interest or expertise - good! Now it's time to start honing it. And if you don't have one, *find one. Now.*

Find your interest and START HONING IT EARLY

If you already have something that you're into, and that you participate in on a demonstrable level, good for you! Now see what *more* you can do to take things even further! Can you start or lead a relevant club? Win an award? Attend a well-reputed course? Whatever it is - do it! Just remember to *focus.* **You are trying to show that you are AWESOME AT <u>ONE THING</u>.** That is all. Everything else is just icing on the cake.

I'm not saying that you're not allowed to be awesome at two things, or three, or four. But before you go for the whole bunch, make sure you're really, really good at **one of them** first. If you're a recruitment-worthy football player, and you *also* happen to be an amazing flutist - wowza!

If you <u>*don't*</u> have a key area of interest, *find one.* Experiment. Put in the work. Remember that *no area is more or less important than any other.* You don't need to be a poet, a baseball player, a chemist, or an architectural genius. You just need to find *something* that *truly* interests you and *pursue it demonstrably.*

If nothing in life interests you...that's a problem beyond the scope of this book.

At this point, there's another question that I'm frequently asked:

How do I find the time?
With all the other demands on your time, how the heck are you supposed to become truly awesome at something outside of school, testing, etc.? You *make it*. The next chapter will show you how.

CHAPTER 19

Cutting Fat and Making Time

"But I'm soooooo buuussssyyyyyyyyy!"
— *EVERY HIGH SCHOOL STUDENT IN AMERICA*

Want the time necessary to keep a high GPA, get good test scores, *and* become an interested, interesting expert in something? Then **cut the fat.**

Most students participate in WAY too many activities that add absolutely NOTHING to their application value.

This is a direct result of the "well rounded myth" that we already discussed. A lot of well-meaning parents sign their kids up for a multitude of random activities in the false belief that these extra activities will make them look "well rounded." They don't. They just make them look *bloated.*

If you want to figure out whether an activity is worth your time, ask yourself ONE question: can <u>anyone</u> do this activity at the level at which I'm doing it? If so, STOP IMMEDIATELY. It's a waste of your time.

Wow! You're a member of 12 clubs? Guess what - *I could sign a turtle up for 12 clubs.*

Oh! You volunteered at the old folks' home twice last year? How *remarkable.*

I'm not saying that clubs and community service are bad - I'm saying that *if you're not going to actually commit to something and demonstrate excellence in and passion for it, then it's a waste of time as far as college applications are concerned.*

College admissions officers are allergic to BS. They've seen it all. Saying that "you're in model UN" means *nothing* to them, because *anyone* can be in model UN. Have you won an award in model UN? Are you a leader within your school's model UN? That's a different story.

Did you complete your mandatory community service? Did you go on a weeklong vacation (I mean...community service trip) to Barbados to build houses? What a humanitarian!

On the other hand, if you've spent 3 hours a week at the old folk's home every single week since freshman year, you've raised money for charity through repeated efforts within your community, and you're the head of your school's PALS program, it probably means that you're *actually interested in philanthropy*, and you're not just using some scummy trick to try and show the school what a good person you are.

Before I get ruthlessly attacked, let me make something clear: **if you're doing something because you genuinely like doing it, or because it genuinely makes you feel good, then more power to you! Life isn't all about getting into college. But if you're doing something just because you think colleges will like it, but you don't really have any interest in doing it, then it's a total waste of your time.**

That's all I'm trying to say. Leave any value judgments at the door.

"But I'm Soooooooooooo Busyyyyyyyyy!!!!!

I won't attempt to trivialize the trials and tribulations of a high school student. But I get a *lot* of people who tell me that there *just isn't enough time in the day* to possibly do everything necessary to craft a competitive application. To which I say: *let's look at the numbers.*

Let's say a high school student has school from 8am to 3pm - a long day.

He has to get up at 7am, which means he needs to be in bed by 11am if he wants to get his eight hours of sleep (which he should).

He's back from school at 3:30.

If he has four hours of homework, which is a lot, and he focuses, which he should, then he can get through it all by 7:30pm.

Build in a 45-minute dinner with the family and a 45-minute phone call with a friend / Facebooking / dedicated screwing around (not to mention the fact that he was at school with his friends for seven hours, during which time he had multiple study breaks, lunch, etc.), and he still has another **two solid hours** to get other stuff done during weekdays.

Every single weekday.

A few more things I need to mention:

1. **He also has the weekends.** 16 hours each day X two days = another 32 hours a week to have fun *and* develop his expertise.
2. **Four hours of homework a night is ridiculous.** Some nights he'll have that much. Some nights he'll have more. Most nights he'll have much less (and be honest - of the four hours during which he's "doing homework," how many are actually spent checking Twitter and texts, grabbing snacks, drifting to the TV in the background, etc.). Also, he'll usually have a lot of time during study hall etc.

The point I'm making here is obvious: even on this pretty ballistic schedule, you still have **42 hours a week to develop an area of expertise!**

That's a lot of time.

Here's where the objection comes in:

Yeah, but I have [ACTIVITY] that takes up a lot of those 42 hours!

And now we've come full circle. *What activity IS that? And is it actually contributing to your college application?* If it's not, and you don't actually enjoy it, then QUIT!!!

Even under extreme circumstances, you should have at least 40 hours a week to devote to developing an expertise *of your choosing*. If that time is being eaten up by activities that AREN'T developing your expertise, then DROP THEM - they are doing absolutely nothing for you.

Here's where people might bring up another objection:

> *Come on, Anthony. There's something to be said for being a generalist! I mean - college asks you to complete lots of disparate, varied activities - don't you want to show the college that you're ready for whatever they throw at you?*

Yes! You do want to show colleges that you're ready for anything - and you do that by *getting good at stuff.* Remember:

Colleges only care about ONE thing: DEMONSTRABLE EXCELLENCE

That's what leads to money and reputational enhancement. If you show colleges that you *participate in lots of activities at a mediocre level,* then what you're telling them is that *you are very good at being mediocre at stuff and signing up for things.*

Anyone who encourages you to invest in meaningless activities that you don't enjoy, aren't good at, and aren't interested in because they show that you're "a good general-ist" or that you're "well rounded" has *absolutely no idea what he's talking about.*

You can **make time** for the things you need to by **taking it back** from the time-wasting activities in which you currently participate. Some are worse than others.

The Main Offenders:

Remember: *any* activity that doesn't *directly contribute* to your *narrative of expertise,* and that you're not wild about, is a complete waste of your time. But these are the absolute worst:

1. **JV Sports.** If you're on the JV basketball team, it is doing less than nothing for your chances of getting into college.
   In fact, even if you're on varsity, *if you're not good enough to get RECRUITED, then it's not really doing anything for your chances of getting admitted.*

If you absolutely love the game, and love the friends you have on the team, then by all means, stick with it. But if you're just doing it because you think it'll help you get into college, then **jump ship.**

Any sports team will take up at least 10 hours/week of your time. If you aren't getting recruited, it won't help with college. So only do it if you really like it - and even then, realize that it's a sacrifice you can make if you need more time.

If you hate sports, but your school requires that you play one, pick the least time-intensive sport possible.

2. **Clubs.** Being a *member* of a club means basically nothing to colleges. I will say this in no uncertain terms:
   If you are the <u>head/founder/president</u> of a club, colleges will find it impressive. If not, you are doing *nothing* for your application.

   Anyone can join any club. High school clubs aren't allowed to kick you out because they don't like you - they aren't fraternities. If you're not a leader/ potential leader of your club, and you don't love being a member, then quit.

   The one exception: if the club has to do directly with your area of expertise, then *maybe* you can stay on - if you have the time. But honestly, if you're not getting some sort of leadership position, just bounce.

3. **Committees/fake leadership positions/BS titles.** If you want to be a world-class photographer, and you're the head of your yearbook's photography department – awesome! If you're the "treasurer" of your yearbook committee, and you're not trying to be an accountant, then just drop it. No one cares.
   Becoming class president is one of the most impressive things you can possibly do. Signing up to be comptroller of your class' brownie sale is not.

   Here's the basic rule on this: *if you were elected to your position by a large group of people, it's probably impressive. If you signed up, it's probably not.*

The Golden Rule: if it doesn't contribute to your narrative, drop it.

Your "narrative" is the story with the blank: "You should let me in because I'm an incredible _____." So if the activities you're pursuing help to back that narrative up, they're probably worth it. If not, they're probably not. Drop them.

There's a lot more to life than getting into college, but don't pretend that you're too busy to make time for the stuff that really matters.

You can get eight hours of sleep a night, conquer your schoolwork, spend time with friends and family every day, exercise, and still commit 30-40 hours of time every week to developing your expertise. And remember: your expertise is something that *you are interested in.* I'm not asking you to join the math club if you hate math. I'm asking you to do something that *you* like. This isn't some massive sacrifice.

Sure, the "thing you like" can't be "eating pizza" or "playing video games" or "hanging out," but if that's all you want out of life, then why go to college anyway? There are plenty of people who didn't go to college who hang out, play video games, and eat pizza all day. You could do it for decades - it would never get old!

But if you want more opportunities for yourself, you'll make the time to develop your expertise. Take a hard look at your schedule, cut the fat, and build in the activities that'll allow you to pursue your interest(s) of choice.

The rest is up to you!

CHAPTER 20

APs and Your Narrative

There are two reasons why most people take AP courses:

1. **Some colleges take high AP scores as college credit, which saves you time and money, and allows you to advance more quickly through the curriculum once you're enrolled.**
    To find out whether the colleges you're interested in take APs for credit, you can use this search tool:

    https://apstudent.collegeboard.org/creditandplacement

    Just know that you need to get *good scores* on your AP exams to get credit. You'll need a 4 or a 5, and a 1 will never cut it. Some colleges don't take AP scores in place of credit at all, and others have different requirements. Do your research and find out if and how your target schools use AP scores to affect your requirements, course load, college costs, etc.

    If you get high AP scores, and *if* your target school(s) allow you to replace credits with those scores, it means that you can skip ahead of the curriculum, save money on course credits, and have an all-around more productive, affordable, and enjoyable college experience.

2. **They make you look smart and raise your weighted GPA.**
    AP classes are called "Advanced Placement" for a reason - they're harder than normal classes. And because they are *standardized*, colleges *know* that they're actually difficult. If you do well in an AP class, and you get a high score on the

corresponding AP exam, then colleges know that you know your stuff. There's no guesswork involved, and admissions officers have a nice, objective metric to work with.

Both #1 and #2 are fantastic reasons. However, first and foremost, know this: you should *never* take an AP course unless you *know* that you'll be good at that subject. If you're an awesome science student, take AP chemistry. If not, don't. Taking an advanced class and getting a cruddy grade isn't impressive. AP classes are only worth it *if you can excel*. If you're a traditionally average math student, taking AP calculus probably isn't a good idea.

Second, know this: you should *never* take an AP *exam* unless you've taken the course. You *are* allowed to take AP exams without taking AP courses, but I wouldn't do it if I were you. AP exams are much harder than their corresponding SAT Subject Tests (in my humble opinion), and if you're going to take them, you should have the class work and experience to back up that decision. Do not take AP exams unless you've taken the classes. Period.

All that being said, there's a third extremely good reason to take AP courses:

3. **High AP scores back up your narrative. They're a way to show that you're really good at whatever you happen to be into.**
    If you're saying that you're extremely into math, you better be taking a calculus AP.

If you're into computers, you should probably take AP Computer Science.

If you're a musician, take AP Music Theory.

If you're into robotics, take AP Physics C: Mechanics.

The full list of courses/exams can be found here:

https://apstudent.collegeboard.org/apcourse

There's a wide variety of AP exams, and there's not a "blank" I can think of that doesn't correspond to at least one of them. If you want *demonstrable expertise,* it doesn't get much demonstrable than a high grade on a standardized test corresponding to that area of expertise.

Colleges want people who are *extremely good at one thing,* and the admissions officers need you to *prove that you are good at it.* If you want to do that, find the most closely related AP course(s) and *work your tail off.*

This is an opportunity that you really can't ignore. If you say that you're passionate about medicine, it will look *really* strange if you haven't taken a single science AP (or if you got bad grades on those APs) - but it will look *awesome* if you've taken a few and crushed them.

That's all I need to say about that. Now let's discuss *the* cornerstone of your narrative: your application essay.

CHAPTER 21

Your Essay (The Big One)

Your essays are the only chance you have to express yourself, in full, to the admissions committee, to show them what you're really like, and to have a real "conversation" with whomever is in charge of reading your applications.

Without your essays, you're just a list of numbers, grades, accomplishments, titles, and extracurricular activities. If you have a really good application, you'll also have strong recommendations – and maybe even a note from an interviewer with a little thumbs up. But your essay is *you*. What's the most important thing you can possibly say about yourself in 650 words - and how will you choose to say it?

In my opinion (and in the opinions of the college experts I deal with on a daily basis), your essay is the ultimate *comparative tool*. If an admissions committee is really up in the air between two students, and doesn't know which one to pick, the essay is almost always the deciding factor.

In other words, if you're a recruited soccer player with amazing grades and scores, you're pretty much an automatic admit. If you have amazing scores and grades, you've won countless awards in your area of expertise, you have glowing recommendations, and a note from an interviewer saying that you're a stand-up guy, you're probably in. But *if the admissions committee is on the fence, then the essay plays an enormous role.* It's the last vanguard against rejection.

In this chapter, I'll show you how to knock it out of the park.

Before we begin, one clarification: this chapter is about the *main* essays that you'll be writing for your applications - the 650-word common-app and/or school-designated essays that matter above all else. The shorter supplementary essays will be covered in the next section.

Your Topic IS Your Essay

A lot of students get nervous about their essays because they think that they're "bad writers." What they really mean is that they don't have amazing *prose* - they can't compose Shakespeare-quality literature at the drop of a hat. Fortunately, that doesn't really matter. *Unless you're applying to college as a <u>writer</u>, admissions officers are much more interested in <u>what you have to say</u> than <u>how you actually say it</u>.*

Yes - you still need proper grammar, spelling, etc. - but you don't need to worry about sounding like an award-winning novelist. You just need to get your point across clearly. The bigger question becomes: *what is your point?*

What are you trying to say about yourself? In the 650 words that you're given to tell admissions officers as much about you as possible, what will you choose?

Fortunately, this is a pretty easy question to answer - provided that your essay does the three things required of any successful college essay. To compose something that won't get you rejected, just make sure that your essay *does its job.*

The Three Key Jobs of a College Application Essay:

1. **Be unique and interesting**
2. **Be *supported* and relevant to your narrative**
3. **Hint at what you'll be able to provide to the college**

Let's take a look at each job in a bit more depth:

1. **Be unique and interesting.** If you want to pick a great essay topic, just ask yourself this:
   "Could ANYONE else in my class write this essay? Or am I the only one who possibly could?"

If even one person in your class could write the same essay that you're planning on writing, then don't write that essay. *Your essay must be unique to you*. It must be as unique as your thumbprint. If you're writing about the fact that you like to stay up late at night, realize that you're describing almost every high school student in America. If you're writing about how hard-working you are...give me a break. But if you're writing about the time that the "guess how many jellybeans are in the jar" contest made you realize that you wanted to be a pediatrician...you might be onto something.

Admissions officers have read *countless* essays. If you want to get their attention, you need to write something *different*. If you write an essay that they feel like they've read 1,000 times before, you're not doing yourself any favors. If you write something that's *unique*, then you'll get their attention - if you write something *interesting*, you'll get their admiration.

But it's not just enough to be interesting - you also have to be **relevant and proven.**

2. **Be *supported* and relevant to your application.** Remember: you have a narrative that you're trying to get across. In one way or another, **your essay MUST support your narrative.** It can do this in one of two ways:

    A) Shed even more light on your area of expertise
    B) Explain a glaring weakness in your application

You might have a really funny story about the time that you had to wrestle an angry deer to save your girlfriend's cat. It's unique - it's interesting. But what the heck does it have to do with you and your narrative? If you want to be a vet, and that was the moment when you realized how fascinating you found animals, and how easily humans could help them with the right training, then it's absolutely perfect. If the answer is "nothing," then it's not a good essay topic.

Pick something that *explains who you are as a person* and that *further demonstrates your interest in and passion for your ONE area of expertise.*

Here's your opportunity to really let your area of expertise shine. No matter what it is that you love, you can use your essay to showcase *why* you love it so much, *how* you became that way, or *what you do* to demonstrate your love for it.

Just be sure that the rest of your application supports the information within your essay! For instance, if you say that you're really into marine biology, and nothing on your application has anything to do with marine biology...huh? If you say that you're a perfectionist, but you have a bad GPA - that's not very convincing. If you talk about how philanthropic you are, but you don't have any community service on your resume...you get the idea.

Use your essay as a way of further explaining your narrative. It's the best way to use it. However, there's one other thing that you can do with your essay: if you have some *glaring* weakness in your application, your essay can do a lot to address it. Let me give you an example:

A student of mine had a pretty good GPA, fantastic SAT scores, and was a budding architect. At the age of seventeen, he'd already won multiple junior architecture awards, been through rigorous college architecture courses, and was applying to the best architecture schools in the country. But there was one huge problem with his application: his grades in Chinese. He had taken Chinese for two years, and he'd never gotten better than a C. He *bombed* Chinese. No matter how hard he worked, he just couldn't get the hang of it.

His essay was about the fact that *because he thought that Chinese characters looked like small, intricately designed buildings, he thought that he'd be able to apply his architectural talents to the language as a whole.* Because he saw everything as an architectural model, he was sure that his brain would help him to decipher Mandarin writing, characters, grammar, etc. The only problem was: it didn't. At all. He was totally confused, and because he has a habit of committing to things even when they're not going well, he stuck with Chinese for two years, *refusing* to believe that he wouldn't be able to apply his architectural mind to the language. He never was. His GPA took a hit as a result. But it taught him that he should just stick with what he knew - true, real architecture - and pursue it to even further extents.

This essay was unique, it was interesting, it was funny as heck, it explained even more about him and his love for architecture, and it *also* explained away his horrible grades in Chinese. To make things even better, *one of his recommendations was from his Chinese teacher* (I'll talk about why this worked so well, and recommendations as a whole, in the next section).

This essay was absolutely flawless. No one else could have written it. It was distinctly *him*. It was well written. It was classy. It was fun. But, above all else, *it had to do with his narrative, and everything he said was backed up*. This is the most important part of your entire essay.

If you take care of these two elements, you're in fantastic shape. There's just *one* more job that your essay needs to perform:

3. **It must hint, ever so slightly, at what you're bringing to the table.**
    Remember: colleges are only interested in *what's in it for them*. Your essay is a great way of letting them know.
    You can't be blatant about this - you can't clobber them over the head. Endings like this will make an admission officer's eyes roll into the back of his head:

    "I'm a hard worker, and I can't wait to take my work ethic to your school, where I'm sure to conquer any challenges ahead of me!"

    Uggggggghhhhh

    "That's why I love writing. And when I'm at your school, you better believe that I'll be taking my love and talent for writing straight to every publication that you have to offer!"

    Cue the sound of me vomiting uncontrollably.

    You don't want these sorts of clumsy, heavy-handed promises. But you want your essay, in and of itself, to *suggest* to colleges that you're the kind of person who has a *passion* for *something*, and who will *keep pursuing that passion*. Remember: all colleges want are kids who **are interested.** If you can demonstrate that you have that passion, intensity, interest, and zeal in your essay, then your essay will *inherently* be promising the college that you're going to bring that interest to the table.

Again, to summarize:

1.   Make it unique and interesting
2.   Make it reflect your specialty
3.   Make sure it demonstrates passion

I realize, of course, that these are all easier said than done. To help steer you in the right direction, I'd first like to address the two kinds of essays that you should *never* write:

Gandhi and Grandpa: The Two Ultimate Sins of College Essay Writing

I've read a lot of college essays in my day. Some have been better than others. But the worst ones, without fail, are what I like to call "Gandhi and Grandpa" essays. Here's an idea of what they both look like:

The Gandhi Essay:

"My personal hero is Gandhi / Martin Luther King Jr. / Mother Teresa / Helen Keller. He/she was an extremely profound person who did lots of good things, and I respect that. He/she helped people, which is very good. I like [insert widely respected person] for all these reasons."

You are *far, far from the only person who respects Martin Luther King, Jr.* These essays are trying to "borrow glory" from famous humanitarians, politicians, and heroes - it's a cheap ploy, and one that admissions officers have seen a thousand times before.

The problem with these sorts of essays isn't that there's something wrong with respecting great figures - it's that they say *nothing* about you. Saying that you respect Helen Keller is like saying that you need water to survive. *Everyone* respects Helen Keller.

Gandhi essays satisfy none of the three requirements of a proper essay. They're not unique - they say that you admire the same people that everyone else does. They don't explain your passion/expertise in any way whatsoever (unless, *maybe, you're an historian?*). And they certainly don't tell the school what you have in store for it. *Do not write this kind of essay.*

The Grandpa Essay:

"The person I model my life after is my grandpa / great uncle / grandma / great aunt. He/she [fought in World War II / was a good person / helped a lot of people / provided for his/her family / was a role model]. He/she is very impressive. Also, he/she did something really remarkable that you should know about. Here it is."

These are even worse than Gandhi essays. They're horrible for all the same reasons. They have *nothing to do with you*. They're just *borrowing glory*. Did your great grandfather fight bravely in World War II? That's incredibly admirable, brave, and remarkable. Unfortunately, you aren't your great grandpa. Did your great uncle discover some remarkable invention? Good for *him*!

Your essays need to be about *you* - not anyone else. This is your *one* chance to really express yourself - don't waste it by describing someone else to the admissions officers.

A Quick Note on Outside Help

Thanks to the high-stakes nature of college admissions, a new industry has popped up: the college essay writing industry. Countless people out there are happy to help you as you go through this process. Just a word of warning:

If you want someone to help you <u>formulate</u> your essay, and <u>edit</u> it for grammar and sentence structure - that's fine. But if someone else actually <u>writes</u> one word of your essay, admissions officers will smell it from a mile away.

This is *your* essay. Have some pride. Express yourself. Say what you want to say about yourself. Don't let someone else do it for you. If you're going to get *help*, that's fine. But the help should be in only two forms:

1.   Asking you the questions necessary to clarify your thinking.
2.   Basic grammatical and structural edits.

Every sentence and every word in your essay should be yours, and yours alone. Not only is it *depressing* and *half-hearted* to let someone else write your essay - it's also really *stupid*. Admissions officers know what a high school student sounds like, and they know what an adult sounds like. They're geniuses at finding discrepancies between you, your background and resume, and the wording in your essay. **Letting someone write your essay for you is the same thing as getting rejected.**

The Basic Structure of a Great College Essay

I can't tell you what to write about. That's on you. However, I can give you a basic framework. Before we begin, know this: you certainly don't have to use this structure. If you already have a good idea for an essay, and you know how you want to express it, go for it! This is simply a tool that you can use if you're having trouble getting started and you want some inspiration.

1. **The hook.** Start your essay with an attention-grabbing, unique line that leaves the reader dying to know a little more. No matter what you're writing about, this is a good practice to follow.

   "I don't know many people who've had to fight a walrus with their bare hands. I've never had to either - but for a brief moment, I thought I might."

   "If you ever have the chance, I recommend eating a wax cheeseburger."

   "For the hundredth time, my mother warned me not to pick up any more Christmas tree tinsel from the street. For the hundredth time, I refused to listen."

   Even if your essay topic isn't funny or exciting, you can still think of some way to start it that grabs the reader's attention and leaves him wanting more. By the way - these are all actual openings to three of my students' college essays, and all of them were accepted to their schools of choice.

2. **The failing.** What's a way in which you screwed up? Discovered a weakness? Describe that to the reader. You're not trying to play the sympathy card - you're simply trying to make yourself human. When did you find a limitation that you needed to face and beat? When did you realize that you needed to improve? What was a huge obstacle that you needed to overcome?

3. **The realization.** What did that failing teach you? What did you learn about the world? About yourself?

4. **The victory.** How did you put that realization into action? How did you take what you learned and use it to better yourself and/or the scenario in which you found yourself?

5. **Conclusion.** Wrap it up. Talk about how you're not perfect, and never will be, but you liked finding a weakness and beating it, and you're looking forward to more challenges.

Again - this template is far from the only one you can use. It's a "mini-Bildungsroman." As far as structures go, you could do a lot worse. But you can do this in a thousand different ways.

Should it be funny or serious? This is up to you. Are you funny? Make it funny. Are you serious? Make it serious. If you're an artistic, poetic person, try to make the essay artistic and poetic. If you're a straightforward, extremely logical person...you get the idea. *The best essays are the ones that most directly reflect your personality. Nothing is better than a real essay written from the heart. Nothing is worse than an essay in which you pretend to be something that you're not.*

When I applied to college, I wanted to be a comedy writer. My essay answered the question: "what's the greatest moral dilemma you've ever faced?" The essay told a fictional story about the time that I went to a dorm "munch" (an event where we all got free food) and found that there was only one slice of pizza left. Even though I knew everyone else wanted it, I took it anyway. Briefly thereafter, I went through a complete existential meltdown. I adopted, and then abandoned, all the major religions, started taking showers with diluted acid and a brillo pad, and finally found solace in nihilism. It was a totally ridiculous essay, and my college advisor thought I was insane. But it was a direct reflection of my style - it was unique to me. It matched my resume - I was the editor of my school's comedy paper, and I repeatedly stated that I wanted to be a comedy writer. And it told the reader what was in store - I was going to write some comedy when I got to college. It's what I was into, and it's what I did.

There's no right or wrong topic, and no right or wrong structure, *so long as you hit the three key criteria, and so long as your essay reflects who you really are as a person.* From there, you're on your own. But if you need a little bit of extra help, I've got you covered.

A Few Resources to Help You Write an Awesome Essay

No one can write *your* essay but *you*. However, there are a few resources that can help to make you even better. Here are my favorites, in no particular order:

1. **Google "Successful College Essays."** Most colleges publish a few examples of their favorite essays every year, along with comments from their admissions officers on why they liked the essays so much.
   Here's an example of a few "essays that worked" from Johns Hopkins:

   http://apply.jhu.edu/apply/essays/

   These are some fantastic essays. In all cases, you'll notice that they contain the "three key elements," and that the admissions officers are always praising them for containing those elements.

   Google is an amazing tool for this, and most schools are very forthcoming with the essays that they like. Do a little searching and you can find successful essays for almost every school in the country.

2. **The Elements of Style by Strunk and White**
   If you don't own this book, *shame on you!* It's the definitive guide on how to write well. Get it, read it, memorize it, and apply it to your essays. It's not just a dry book on grammar - it teaches you amazing stylistic and structural tricks to help keep your essay fresh.

3. **Give your essay to people and ask them to rip it apart.**
   Don't take it to your friends, family, etc. and ask them "what they think." Take it to people and ask them *what they HATE about it.* Tell them that you don't want praise, or general comments. You want *specific things that they DON'T like.*

   I do this with my writing, with business plans, with ad copy, with my software - with pretty much everything. It sounds really pessimistic and masochistic, but it's actually the *best* thing you can do if you want honest, useful criticism. Having someone tell you that your essay is "great" might feel good, but it's no help. If you open the door for real criticism, and *demand* negative feedback, you'll get the really good stuff. You don't always have to use it, but if multiple people hate the same thing, it's a darn good sign that you need to make a change.

4. **Spunk and Bite by Arthur Plotnik.**
    Another favorite. This book will show you how to turn ordinary, boring prose into fascinating, fast-paced reading. This can turn any writer into a great writer.
5. **Word Up! by Maria Johnston.**
    I may have saved the best for last. This book is freaking amazing. Read it, live it, love it. Even if you don't learn anything from it (you will), it's strangely entertaining considering how dry the subject material is supposed to be.

What do you have to say for yourself?

Follow the simple guidelines above and you'll be well on your way toward an amazing college essay. Express yourself, be unique, continue your narrative, and show the school what you have to offer. Look to other essays for inspiration. Get your hands on as many writing guides as you possibly can. Look for honest criticism. And, above all else, *be yourself.* Colleges want to hear from *you, and not anybody else.*

With the essay out of the way, we've covered every element of _you_ that colleges care to know. Believe it or not, we're basically done with the entire process! In the next section, we're just going to do a bit of housekeeping. And for that, we go the final section of this book: **The Application.**

Section Five: The Application

You know - that thing you actually have to turn in.

CHAPTER 22

Supplemental Essays

ost colleges now accept the common application. Some don't. To figure this out, do the following:

1. Go here: https://www.commonapp.org/. Spend some time learning about the common app. If your applications are due soon, sign up and make a free account.
2. Go here: https://apply.commonapp.org/createaccount

You can search colleges and figure out which ones are on the common app (and which ones aren't).

The common app is nice - it lets you fill in all the mundane blanks (name, address, social security number, etc.) one time, rather than for each school on your list. It also has one major essay that can be sent to all the schools on your list - it kills a lot of birds with one stone. And we all hate birds. But whether or not your colleges are all on the common app or not, you can be almost certain of one thing:

At least one of the colleges you apply to will require supplemental essays.

Supplemental essays are the shorter, school-specific essays required by almost every school in the country. If you want an example of these essays, check this out:

http://undergrad.admissions.columbia.edu/apply/writing-supplement

That was found by searching "Columbia essay requirements" in Google. You can go through the same process for every school on your list to figure out what supplements they require (just remember: if you're doing this far in advance, the essay topics will probably change by the time you actually apply. You're just doing this to see *if* they require supplements, how many, and what style they're in. Don't worry about actually writing them that far in advance).

These essays serve a *very* different purpose from the "main essays" that we covered in the last chapter. Once you understand what they're for, you'll quickly understand how to write them well.

The Only Two Reasons Colleges Want You to Write Supplemental Essays:

1. **To prove that you'll attend if they let you in**
2. **To prove that you have a lot to offer to that school, specifically**

Both are equally as important. Let's look at both in a bit more detail.

1. **To prove that you'll attend if they let you in.**
   If you read the Columbia supplements above, and any supplementary essay topics, you'll find the same theme: they are extremely egotistic. "Why do you like us?" "Why do you want to go here?" "What do you think is great about Columbia?"

   Requiring these sorts of essays is actually very smart on their part. If they didn't require supplements, what would stop someone with a bit of extra money from applying to 200 extra schools? Just drop the extra $75 per application and presto - you can apply to all the best colleges in the country with no effort or thought.

   If they allowed this to happen, they'd be flooded with insincere applications. At first, you might think that this would be good for them - they'd get to boast about a lower acceptance rate. But it's not worth it. Remember: more important than *acceptance rate* is *ratio of applicants accepted to applicants attending*. That is the holy grail of application statistics, and if every student in the country applied to every college, it would *not* be good.

Admissions officers are already overburdened. They have enough work, and enough tough decisions to make, without handling thousands of totally insincere applications. Furthermore, every insincere applicant who they let in will take the spot of a sincere applicant who they have to reject. It would screw *everything* up if they didn't require these essays.

Therefore, **the most important job of your supplemental essays is to prove that you have an actual interest in that school, in particular, and that you're dying to go.**

How do you prove this? *Research.*

If you want to write an amazing supplemental essay, mention details about the school that are SPECIFIC to the school, take MORE THAN ONE MINUTE OF RESEARCH TO DISCOVER, and that HAVE TO DO WITH YOUR PARTICULAR NARRATIVE.

Here's an example of an absolutely rubbish answer to: "Tell us why you want to attend Columbia:"

I want to attend Columbia because it is such a well-esteemed institution. Your college is famous for its amazing teaching staff, resources, and history. Your curriculum, in particular, is well known as being one of the most challenging and profoundly educational in the world. Furthermore, your position in the heart of New York City is inspiring and exciting. Columbia is, and always has been, my dream school.
The rubbish radar just got set off, and anti-rubbish cruiser missiles are flying in to blow up your application and send the wreckage into the nearest trashcan.

You need to mention *specifics. Every* college thinks that it has a great curriculum, beautiful campus, amazing teachers, etc. What *about* those things do you like the most? Which elements? You could send this supplemental essay to any school in the country.

Do your research. Find out what you really like about the school. Talk about it in your essays. Convince them. I didn't ask you to do all that research in section one because I'm a fan of long, arduous tasks - I asked you to do it because it plays a part in every other element of the application process. If you can't name a few specific, awesome things about the schools to which you're applying, why are you applying in the first place?

2. **Prove that you have a lot to offer that school, specifically.**
   Almost every supplemental essay will ask: "why do you want to go here?" But there's a sneaky hidden message. What they also want to know is, "what will you do for us when you get here?"

That's the unwritten question that they *really* want you to answer. The best applicants are the ones who know this, and who build an *offer* into all their supplements.

If you combine your *narrative*, your *talents*, and the *elements of the school that will allow you to exercise your talents once you're there,* you're going to craft flawless supplements every time. Here's a basic template for how this works:

A) **Intro - Here's the thing I'm most interested in in life.**
B) **Here's something you offer, specifically, that complements my interest.**
C) **Here's how I'll use that thing.**
D) **Repeat B and C to fill up the required space.**
E) **Conclusion: "I can't wait to go!"**

Every single one of your supplements should follow that model. Will it take a bit of work? Absolutely. But it's well worth it.

Here's an example of the Columbia supplement again, following these rules:

My whole life, I've wanted to be a doctor. As a result, many in my family don't understand my fixation with Columbia. "Wouldn't you rather go to a school with a dedicated pre-med program?" they often ask. But they haven't done the research that I have, and they don't understand the unsurpassed opportunities that your college provides to an aspiring doctor.

While you don't offer any specific pre-med programs, your biology, chemistry, and psychology departments are unsurpassed. I've read multiple books by [professor X], This Book Title being my favorite, and I've dreamed of the opportunity to learn under him. I have only one goal in college: to learn as much about science, medicine, and psychology as I possibly can. Between [this class I want to take] and [this other field of study offered specifically by Columbia], I can't imagine a better place to hone my craft and improve my scientific and medical reasoning skills.

Furthermore, Columbia's access to its own medical school resources, proximity to world-class hospitals, Mt. Sinai in particular, and opportunities for medical internships are superior to those offered by any other school on my list.

etc., etc., etc.

See what's going on here? Anyone who reads this is going to know, for a fact, that you've done your homework. Columbia isn't just some "high ranking name" on your list that you threw on for fits and giggles - it's somewhere that you *really* want to go. If they let you in, you'll show up. Furthermore, you've proven something equally as important: that when you get to Columbia, you're going to be a beast. They know you'll rip your classes apart. They know you like learning. And, if the rest of your application backs up what you're saying here, then you're going to be a darn good doctor.

You just might get into a really good medical school. That helps their reputation.

You just might perform some important research while you're at Columbia. That helps their reputation.

You just might become a successful doctor and make a lot of money. That helps their reputation.

You just might give some of that money back to Columbia. That makes them money.

I think I've made my point. This entire process can be boiled down to the following steps:

1. Do your research. Figure out *everything* about the schools you're applying to - why you want to go, what they have to offer you, what you have to offer them, and what you'll do when you show up.
2. Research the supplemental requirements of every school to which you're applying.
3. Write your essay following the "here's what you have (specifically), here's how I'll use it to make you money and enhance your rep" formula.
4. If you're going to write a vague essay, or fail to do your research, then don't apply to that school at all. You'll get the boot.

Speaking of killing lots of birds, I want to address another element of your application that'll be quite easy to handle after reading this chapter: your interviews.

CHAPTER 23

Interviews

As I mentioned earlier on, interviews are a fantastic idea. But they are only fantastic if they're done right. Fortunately, doing them right is pretty darn easy - *interviews follow the EXACT same principles that supplementary essays do.*

You only have two jobs during your interview(s):

1. Show how interested you are in the school.
2. Show the interviewer what you'll do when you get there.

Your college interviews are NOT the same thing as job interviews. You don't get an "accept" or "reject" note when you're done. In fact, many colleges don't even consider interviews as part of their admissions criteria (or at least, they say they don't - if you break down crying in the middle of the interview for no reason, you might have a problem).

A great interview boils down to one piece of advice:

Ask questions that you can't Google, and keep the focus on the school.

That's all there is to it. This is actually the same piece of interview advice that I give to people applying for *jobs* as well - it's equally as effective. The basic idea being this:

Everyone is more interested in themselves than they are in strangers. If you show your interest in other people, ask them questions about themselves, and demonstrate your eagerness to help them, you'll make a great impression. If you blather on about yourself, you're not impressing anybody.

When you hear the word "interview," you probably imagine yourself sitting across a desk, being grilled on what books you've read, what your IQ happens to be, why you're worthy of the school, etc. This isn't what happens at all. Instead, it'll probably go something like this:

"Thanks for visiting us, Joe. What brings you here today?"
Some of the questions you can expect:
"So, tell me about yourself. What are your interests?"
"What do you do in your free time?"
"Where did you grow up?"
"Do you have any brothers or sisters?"
"What interests you about our school?"

These aren't "grilling" questions. You're not being tested. **Interviewers are *there for YOU.*** They're interviewing you mostly to answer *your* questions and to teach *you* more about the school - not to give you a grade from A-F. School interviews are *extremely friendly events*. There's absolutely no need to be nervous.

Before we go on, I actually want to offer one more piece of advice:

Be 100% honest. And be yourself.

This is good advice in life in general. But it's especially important during these interviews. Don't ever lie, or tell half-truths, or stretch the truth, just to impress your interviewer. There's absolutely *nothing* to gain from doing this. You have zero reward, and the risk is that you end up looking like a lying, dishonest jerk. If the interviewer asks you what your favorite book is, you don't have to respond with War and Peace. Do you really like The Hunger Games? Then just say that. If it's your favorite book, it's your favorite book. *Be yourself.* If the interviewer asks if you play chess, and you don't, say "no." Because that's the truth. You shouldn't have to "think of" any answers, because they should all be in your mind already.

You don't need to prepare any *answers* for the interviewer, because you'll just be telling him or her the truth. The only things you need to prepare are some *questions*.

If you want to "impress" an interviewer, collect a few questions about the school that *you couldn't easily answer on Google*. Try to weave them into the conversation (usually, he/she will specifically ask, "do you have any questions for me?" - if you don't, it's a sign that you're not really that interested in the school).

Are there any other politics-related clubs on campus *beyond* the ones that you found online? Ask! Have they ever partnered with any culinary schools in the area? Check it out! Who's the best English teacher on campus in his opinion? See if he knows!

All you're doing is asking questions that *you actually want answered*, that will help you to further ascertain your interest level in the school. That is all. So long as your questions are thoughtful, sincere, reflect your interests, and are not easily Google-able (i.e. "how many students are there on campus?"), you're good to go!

Dress Code, Handshake, and All That Other BS

Recently, an article came out about *how to dress for your college interviews*. The kids in the feature, put together by a college consultant based out of CT, were basically wearing the season's J Crew catalogue. This is the sort of thing that gives my entire industry a bad name.

If you want to make a good impression, **be honest, be sincere, and ask questions that show your interest in the school**. That's it. That's all there is to it.

Worried about your dress? Don't be. If you're a guy, make sure to shower in the morning, and try to wear something with a collar. If you're a girl, wear the same thing you'd wear to an event that your grandma was attending. That's about as much thought as you need to put into it. Obviously, you don't want to wear a T-shirt with a weed leaf on it or a flat-brimmed baseball cap that says "F U Dude" on the front, but if your dress isn't obviously offensive, you're fine.

Worried about your handshake, or your entrance, or exit? Don't be. Give a firm handshake and keep eye contact whenever you can.

Are you a nervous person? Do your hands sweat? So what. Interviewers are used to it. There's no "sweaty palms!" sticker that'll get tacked onto your application. I'm sure the interviewer has shaken 1,000 hands 10X sweatier than yours.

Just go in there and *be yourself.* I cannot overemphasize the simplicity of this process. The *only* way that you can mess this up is by trying to be someone who you're not.

What's the worst thing that can happen during your interview? You don't make a big splash. It won't really matter. What's the best thing that can happen? You'll learn a lot more about the school - a place where you want to spend the next four years of your life - by asking interesting questions that you haven't been able to answer so far. What's the second best thing that can happen? The interviewer might make a little note on your application that says, "Good kid! Definitely into the school!" That's about it.

They're an important way to demonstrate your interest in the school, and to find out more about it. The interview is a tool for *you* to learn more about a *potential opportunity that YOU may want to pursue - act accordingly!*

CHAPTER 24

Supplementary Materials

Some colleges allow you to submit "supplementary materials" along with your application. Here are some of the things you may (or may not) be allowed to submit:

- DVDs of your athletic performance
- Samples of art you've produced
- Samples of creative writing that you've made
- Websites you've designed or apps you've created
- Short films you've directed
- etc.

The idea is this: some colleges realize that not everything impressive about you can be slotted into the neat categories they've provided in their applications. Therefore, they'll let you show them some stuff that's "outside the normal boundaries" and consider it during the application process.

If you have something like this that you want to submit, keep reading. If not, skip to the next chapter.

There are only a few things that you need to know about this entire process:

1. **Only certain schools allow it. You need to find out which do.**
   How? Easily: Google.

Just go online and type the following:

"Does [school] allow supplementary material in their application?"

A few clicks will get you to the admissions website, where they'll let you know *if they consider ANY supplementary materials at all*, and, if so, *what sorts of materials they'll accept.*

If the schools on your list *don't* accept supplementary materials, it's not the end of the world. If they *do*, know this:

2. **These materials will ONLY be reviewed in stage three of your application, and only as a last-ditch resort.**

If you've developed a really cool app, but you have horrible grades and test scores, your demo video on YouTube won't do a thing for you.

Don't expect these materials to get you any sort of red carpet voucher, or to "set you apart from the pack." In the case of college admissions, *less is more.* If you need a DVD or a portfolio of paintings to tell colleges why you're impressive, it means that you couldn't do it in your application alone, which is a bit of a red flag.

Admissions officers are already busy. By submitting supplementary materials, you're asking them to do more work. Therefore, you should only submit this sort of thing if it's *relevant.*

3. **These materials need to be relevant to your narrative.**
If your entire application revolves around your desire to be a painter, then by all means, send some pictures of your paintings! If you want to be a director, and you have a YouTube link to a short film you directed, send it! If you're a recruited tennis player, and you have a video of your best serves - send it. If you're an aspiring journalist, and you had an article published in a local magazine, clip it out and mail it right along. All of these things make sense.

But *for the love of God*, DO NOT SUBMIT SUPPLEMENTARY MATERIAL THAT DOESN'T HAVE TO DO WITH YOUR MAIN STORY.

This is a huge distraction, a pain in the neck, and makes you look absolutely **desperate.**

If you're saying that you want to be a doctor, and then you send a portfolio of some paintings you've done - what?

If you want to be a journalist, and then you send photos of the award-winning sculptures you made in 9th grade - huh?

If you're trying to be a chemist, and you send a hilarious comedy sketch that you and your friends made last year...

You get the idea. Remember: **colleges don't want well-rounded students.** Sending them random stuff that they have to look through is *not* going to help you. Only send it if it supports your narrative, and *for no other reason.* And if the college says they don't want it or won't consider it, don't bother. Sending it regardless of their wishes is a huge red flag, and shows that you either haven't done your research or don't care what the school thinks - or both.

That's all there is to it!

CHAPTER 25

Getting Good Recommendations

As we near the end of this book, you might notice something: I repeat the same point *over and over and over again.* **Craft a single narrative and stick with it.** That's the best way to avoid getting rejected and end up in the "admit" pile. I repeat it so often because, once your grades and test scores are high enough, *it's the only thing that really matters.*

So it'll be no surprise to learn that this chapter addresses the same theme. Want great recommendations? Find the two teachers who'll support your narrative. Fortunately, this is easy to do. But before you focus on your narrative, you need to focus on something else: your quality as a human being.

Recommendations are the "testimonials" of your college application

My business partner and I spent a lot of time analyzing the data from my websites. We like to figure out where people spend their time and what matters most to them. And, not surprisingly, everyone who visits both my software and my tutoring sites makes a beeline directly to my testimonials page. Why? Because *testimonials are the most honest, trustworthy pieces of information you can possibly find.* I can say all I want about myself and my software, but I'm biased. My students and their parents, on the other hand, have no stake in my success - they can trash me, leave lukewarm comments, or praise me - they mean whatever they say, and they have no incentive to "puff me up."

Yelp is the first place most people go to figure out whether a restaurant is worthwhile. If you want to try a new pair of headphones, you check the reviews on Amazon. Very rarely do you read the restaurant's homepage, or the manufacturer's description, to figure out how good something is.

The things that your teachers say about you are the most direct, honest, and revealing elements of your entire application. They're pure trustworthiness. Admissions officers don't have to wonder whether they're inflated or dishonest or misleading. Therefore, they're extremely important. They're the only part of your application that really reflects *your quality as a person.*

Fortunately for you, you don't even need to write your recommendations - your teachers do all the work for you! All you need to do is **ask the right teachers.**

Who Should You Ask?
This is a very simple process. The first part is the most important:

1. **Only ask teachers who like and respect you, and who you know will write GLOWING recommendations.**
   This might seem like obvious advice, but you'd be blown away by how many students request applications from teachers who don't like them very much. If a teacher hates your guts, he simply won't write a recommendation for you (or he'll write one and tear you apart). You're obviously not going to ask for a rec from someone you don't like.

   But **the worst kind of recommendation is a LUKEWARM recommendation.**

   After all the work you've put into this process, and all the flattering things that you've tried to say and suggest about yourself, imagine a college admissions officers reading this:

   "Terry was in my calculus class. He did pretty good work. Other kids seemed to like him. Not a bad kid. I gave him an A-, and I think he could have gotten an A or an A+, but he showed up and did what was required."

YIKES.

That is bad, bad news. It tells the admissions officers that *you don't make an impression.* Remember: colleges want kids who have **demonstrable expertise and passion.** If you're making such a lukewarm impression on your teachers, where's your passion? It certainly wasn't contagious.

Most colleges require one recommendation from a "humanities" teacher and one from a "math or science" teacher. Make sure you ask the teacher in those subjects who LOVED you most.

When I was in high school, I *bombed* physics. I was horrible at it. It didn't really click. But my professor *loved* me. Why? Because I worked my butt off. I've never tried so hard in any class, ever in my life. I went all out every day, showed up for every after-class review session, asked her insightful questions, and really pushed myself. She couldn't give me good grades - I didn't get them on her tests and quizzes. But she knew how hard I tried, and she saw my work ethic, and she was the one who wrote my recommendations. While she couldn't *show* me the recommendation, she let me know that it was "very, very good."

We all have teachers who love us. And this love has little to do with our actual grade in their classes. It can be an A or an F - it doesn't matter. You just want to pick the teachers who are *oozing with enthusiasm for you.* Nothing else will do. Don't pick a teacher unless you know he or she will spend at least an hour *agonizing* over your recommendation to make it as good as possible. That's the first criteria.

2. **Ask professors who will support your narrative in some way or another.** Remember the two messages I told you to convey in your main application essay? Either:

A) Show why your strengths are so strong
    Or
B) Explain away your weaknesses

Your teachers have the power to do precisely the same things. Ideally, you'll get one teacher to handle one of these tasks, and one teacher to handle the other. **You cannot, should not, and must not tell your teachers what you want them to write - or even suggest concepts. This is the most impolite, ridiculous thing you can possibly do. Instead, you need to pick teachers who you KNOW will say the things that you want them to say automatically.**

For instance, let's say that you want to be a journalist. One of your recommendations should be from an English teacher who absolutely loved you. You want them to explain your skills in English, how great a writer you are, etc. That supports the narrative. The other recommendation could be from a math teacher who gave you a bad grade, but who still respected you as a person, and who thinks very highly of you - but just doesn't think you're innately talented at math.

Just two things to keep in mind:

1. **The "fanciness" of your teachers doesn't matter.** You don't need the teacher who teaches the most "well-respected course," nor does your teacher need to be extremely eloquent. My physics teacher spoke English as a third language. But the enthusiasm was real, regardless of her grammar.
2. **The grades you got in that teacher's class don't matter, so long as he/she supports your narrative and/or explains away a weakness.** If a teacher gave you a good grade - great! If not - it's not a problem - *so long as there was a good reason why you got that bad grade that explains something important about you, and that's presented in a positive light.*

That's all there is to it.

Pick teachers who love you, and who will back up your narrative by explaining how awesome/interested you are in the thing you love and, maybe, why you didn't knock the thing(s) you don't love out of the park. You'll know what teacher to pick far better than I will. But so long as you follow these rules of thumb, you'll end up with the best possible recs!

CHAPTER 26

Avoid Fluff

n the spirit of being meta, I'll make this chapter incredibly short.

When you fill out your application, don't include anything that isn't significant. It's just distracting.

College admissions officers are good at sniffing out fluff and "ploys."

It's better to leave a section blank than to fill it with some obvious "throwaway" that doesn't really matter to you.

Let your narrative shine through. Let admissions officers focus on the stuff that you've truly devoted yourself to. If you include information that doesn't really say much, it'll just take the spotlight away from the stuff that you really want admissions officers to see.

Did you do one trip, one time, to the old-folk's home during your sophomore year? Just leave "community service" blank.

Did you play a term of intramural ultimate Frisbee? Just leave the athletics section alone. *When in doubt, throw it out.* Your application should be as crisp, clear, and focused as possible.

That is all.

CHAPTER 27

Applying Early

Before we're done, there's one last thing I'd like to address: *should you apply early?* If so, what's the best way to do it?

Applying early comes with a whole lot of benefits, but it also carries its fair share of risks. Before we answer this question, we first need to distinguish between **early decision** and **early action**.

Early Decision: You can only apply early decision to one school. If you're accepted, you *have to go*. You must withdraw all applications from all other schools. If you go back on your Early Decision commitment, you'll need to give up a sizeable enrollment deposit.

If you're rejected, you'll usually be put into the pool for regular admissions automatically. If not, you'll be able to apply for regular admission free of charge (but don't get your hopes up).

Almost all ED schools allow you to apply to *only that school*. *Some* allow you to apply to other schools so long as those schools offer Early Action. But the rules don't change - if you get into the ED school, you have to attend.

Early Action: About 15% of schools in the country offer EA. You can apply to multiple Early Action schools at once. If you're accepted, you don't have to commit - you can wait until the spring deadline to make your decision, and compare all the other EA schools that accepted you. There's also something called **Single-Choice Early Action**. If you use this option, you're only allowed to apply to ONE school early - but, if they let you in, you can also apply regular admission to *more* schools if you choose to do so. You don't have to give your offer until the spring. You'll have time to weigh financial aid options, other acceptance offers, etc.

If you're rejected, it's the same deal as ED for both kinds of Early Action.

Early Action is a way, way better deal than Early Decision. It's non-binding, allows you to cast a wider net, get better financial aid options, and more. So why would someone ever choose Early Decision? **Because your dream school might be early Decision, and not early Action.**

That's the only answer.

Remember that whole thing about colleges *really* wanting to know whether or not you're going to attend if they let you in? Well - Early Decision is a *guarantee*. If you apply Early Decision, you're telling the school, in no uncertain terms, that if they let you in, it's happening.

Early Action is more of a *strong suggestion*. It shows a bit more commitment than regular applications - but not by too much.

You can use this tool to figure out which schools are Early Decision and Early Action:

http://www.collegedata.com/cs/search/college/college_search_tmpl.jhtml

Type in a college's name and hit "search." When you see the college listed, click on its name, highlighted in blue. Once you get to the next page, click the "Admission" tab under the school's name. Here's Harvard's:

http://www.collegedata.com/cs/data/college/college_pg02_tmpl.jhtml?schoolId=444

This page will show you plenty of nifty data about the admissions scenario of every school in the country, including SAT Subject Test requirements, SAT vs. ACT requirements, etc.

But if you scroll down, you'll see whether the school *offers* Early Decision or Early Action, and *which one(s) they offer.* Yes - I said "one(s)." **Some schools offer BOTH Early Decision AND Early Action - the point being that Early Decision shows *extreme commitment.*** Schools like that.

You'll also find their deadlines for early applications. *Write these down and put them on your calendar or next to the college's name on your list.* You don't want to have to look it up again.

Do this for every single school on your list.

Now that you know **what ED and EA are**, **which colleges offer them**, and **when you need to decide by**, it's time to look at the advantages and pitfalls of applying early.

Why Do People Apply Early?

There are actually only *three* reasons why people do this.

1. **They want to get this process over with.** As you'll learn shortly, this isn't always a very good idea. Yes, the application process is stressful, and sometimes it's tempting to rip off the Band-Aid, but unless you *really* know where you want to go, there are certain advantages to waiting.

2. **They're 100% sure where they want to go.** Your mom and dad both went to Boston University. It's your dream school. You're obsessed with it. You go to the campus every day to admire the architecture. You can't imagine yourself anywhere else. If that's you - sure, apply ED to BU.

3. **They're showing the school that they're more committed.** This is the most logical reason to apply early. If you send in an early application - *especially* an Early Decision application - you're letting the school know that you mean business. You wouldn't be applying early if you weren't into it. As we've already discussed, this is a big deal for them. Of course, you still need to be good enough for them, but it's nice to let them know that they're good enough for you, too. What's the only problem here? **The early applicant pool is usually more competitive than the regular applicant pool, so the positive effects of early application are counterbalanced by the more competitive applicant pool.**

All in all, I'd say that #3 is sort of a wash. There are other ways of showing a school that you mean business, and we've already covered all of them.

Before we get into the drawbacks of early applications, two quick notes:

If your early application is *rejected*, then you are not getting into that school next year. It's over. You can always apply for transfer in later years, but not this time around.

If your early application is *deferred*, it means that your application goes into the regular admission pool. You avoided getting rejected, which is nice. But the school needs to see more. They'll be waiting to see your senior year grades, new test scores, new accomplishments, etc. You have some time to spiff up your application - and if you're really interested in that school, you should. Getting deferred isn't a death sentence, but it's not a great sign, either. If you get deferred, you still have a *chance*, but don't count on it unless you make big improvements to your previous application.

Why SHOULDN'T You Apply Early?

There are plenty of reasons, actually. I'm all for early applications - the sooner you can put this process behind you, the better. But there are many disadvantages to doing it:

1. **It rushes your decisions.** You have less time to research, tour campuses, etc. Of course, this should have been taken care of far earlier, but still - the more time, the better. Where you attend college is one of the most important decisions of your life - don't rush it because you "just want to get it all over with." This is foolish, short-term thinking at its finest.
2. **If you apply ED, you're marrying a school.** Unless you are absolutely, 100%, positively sure that you want to go there, don't do it. It would be really foolish to make a complete commitment to a school that you don't actually want to attend.
3. **If you apply ED, you're also taking a huge financial risk.**
   There's one exception to the "full commitment" rule: if you get accepted ED, and you don't get offered the financial aid package you're looking for, you're allowed to decline the school's offer completely and then apply to other schools.

This really stinks. It means that you got into your dream school, but that it didn't matter. You still need to apply everywhere else, and you're turning down an acceptance. It's a horrible feeling. If financial aid is going to be important to you, ED is very risky. EA and regular admission allow you to compare aid packages, etc. before making any decisions. In fact, I'd say that **if you're relying on financial aid, you simply shouldn't apply ED.** It's a bad decision.

4. **The applicant pool is more competitive.** Already mentioned, but worth saying again. The people who apply ED and EA usually have knowledgeable parents and/or advisors helping them with their applications, which usually means that they have better all-around applications. That's something to keep in mind.

5. **No chance to improve grades, test scores, etc.** If you're applying early, you're giving yourself less time to show off a stellar senior fall GPA, improve your SAT or ACT scores, get better Subject Test scores, etc. If you're already confident in your stats and accolades, then this doesn't matter. *If you feel like your application needs a bit more work, and you think a little GPA, test score, or "credentials" boost would make a big difference, then applying early will be a bit of a disaster.*

6. **Applying early can lead to rushed *applications*.** I mean the actual application(s) themselves. If you know where you want to go, and you've put in the research, that's great. But you have way less time to finish your essays, get recommendations, write supplemental essays, etc. *If you plan in advance, this isn't that big a deal.* If you're scrambling to write essays, ask for recs, do research, finish supplemental essays, etc., you're going to end up submitting a cruddy application. Not the best idea.

The decision is up to you

No pun intended. If you're 100% sure where you want to go, and you're not counting on financial aid, go for Early Decision (if necessary). If not, stick with EA and regular decision. And with that, we've come to our journey's end. There are just a few more loose ends to tie up.

Final Words and Next Steps

hope you enjoyed reading this book half as much as I enjoyed writing it! <u>Why You Get Rejected</u> has been years in the making, and I've tried to provide you with the most comprehensive, honest, and easy-to-use college admissions book I could possibly write.

No matter where you end up at college, you'll be able to learn, grow, and explore unique opportunities with like-minded, awesome people. The college you choose just determines *what* you'll learn, *which opportunities* you'll explore, and *which people you'll be learning and exploring with.* Hopefully this book has given you the tools you need to find the right one.

Every chapter in this book is *action-based.* If you haven't already taken the steps recommended in each chapter, I'd recommend starting from scratch, skimming each chapter again, and then following through on the advice provided in the proper order. There's not a single random recommendation in here - every piece of advice is battle-tested. Follow all of it and your life will be a lot easier - I promise.

I want to thank you for reading my book - it means a lot to see how many people have already requested it and put its advice into practice, and I'm thrilled to know that you're one of them. I wish you all the best in the application process, and I hope that this guide will get you through unscathed!

Looking for more? I have a TON of free, awesome resources for college applications and test prep over at https://GreenTestPrep.com. Swing by and check

it out! And remember that you can use the code "WYGRcode" to get $25 off my online SAT and ACT prep program if you decide to use it.

Also, if you liked the book, and you want to do me the world's biggest, share it with your friends! Again, thanks so much for reading! If you ever need anything or have any questions, feel free to reach out and get in touch at Support@`ays make sure to reply!

Good luck with everything, and *don't forget to have some fun!*

Best Wishes,

Anthony-James Green
Founder and Creator: Green Test Prep: https://greentestprep.com